WH FISH?

FISH?

A BUYER'S GUIDE TO TROPICAL FISH

Essential advice from a team of experts

INTERPET PUBLISHING

ISBN 10   1 84286 119 0
ISBN 13   978 1 84286 119 6

Credits

Created and compiled:
Ideas into Print, Claydon,
Suffolk IP6 0AB, England.

Design and prepress: Stuart
Watkinson, Ayelands, Longfield,
Kent DA3 8JW, England.

Principal photography: Geoff
Rogers © Interpet Publishing
(see also Credits page 208)

Production management:
Consortium, Poslingford, Suffolk
CO10 8RA, England.

Print production: Sino Publishing
House Ltd., Hong Kong.

Printed and bound in China.
This reprint 2008

The star rating ★★★★★

The star rating offers a guide to the relative price you can expect to pay for each species. The actual cost in relation to the star rating is provided at the start of each group section. Some fish may have two ratings, representing the variable cost based on their size and source. For instance, a large mature fish may cost more than a young juvenile of the same type. Whilst this guide is as accurate as possible, prices can change depending on availability, popularity, and ease of breeding.

Tank dimensions are quoted in length x width x depth.

Authors

Mary Bailey (Cichlids) is an experienced fishkeeper and author, acknowledged internationally for her work on cichlids.

Nick Fletcher (Barbs) is a former editor of Practical Fishkeeping Magazine and writes on tropical and coldwater fishes.

Ian Fuller (Catfishes) is a former tropical fish judge, author and long term fish breeder, specialising in Corydoradinae catfishes.

Richard Hardwick (Oddballs) is a respected aquarist and avid 'oddball' collector. He writes extensively for aquarist magazines.

Peter Hiscock (Characins; Danios; Loaches & Sharks) has written several books. His special interests include fish behaviour.

Pat Lambert (Livebearers) has bred aquarium fish for many years and is highly regarded in the aquatic magazine world.

John Rundle (Rainbowfishes) is an accomplished fishkeeper and breeder, book author and contributor to aquarist magazines.

Andrew Smith (Anabantoids) specialises in labyrinthfish and is species information officer of the Anabantoid Association of Great Britain.

Kevin Webb (Killifishes) is an active member of the Killifish Association, an experienced fish judge and keen aquatic photographer.

Introduction

Choosing which fish to keep in your aquarium can be a bewildering experience, with literally hundreds of common species to choose from. When a benign-looking fish turns into a bully or predatory fish in the home aquarium, it is often the first experience a fishkeeper has of the wide diversity of behaviour of these wonderful creatures. To help avoid such problems, this book describes a representative selection of popular fish from each fish group, allowing you to decide which types of species are suitable for your aquarium. To provide the best possible advice, each section is written by an expert in the hobby and the fish group under discussion. Each fish featured in the book has a general profile, alongside the essential information you need to ensure that it will thrive in the aquarium. What size will it grow to? How does it behave around other fish? What does it eat? Will it breed in my tank? Where does it come from? How many should I have? – these are just a few of the questions you should ask yourself when buying any fish, and are all answered for each fish in this book. With the advice provided you can create an active, healthy mix of shoaling fish, solitary species, bottom, midwater and surface-dwellers to create your community aquarium.

Just as important as choosing the right species is the ongoing care you provide them. To help achieve this, each fish description includes information on preferred water conditions, the right aquarium decor and ideal foods.

Fish are creatures of diverse habits, and even with the best advice some problems do occur, but the information provided in this book should help to keep such difficulties to a minimum, leaving you free to enjoy the rewards of a lively, interesting, and peaceful aquarium.

Contents

In this listing, the common name of each fish is followed by its scientific name. In sections featuring more than one group of fishes, the species are presented in A-Z order of scientific name within each group.

▼ *Discus have been bred into many colour forms, including red and orange strains.*

52 - 83

Catfishes

▲ *The emerald catfish is well named
for its metallic green body colour.*

Contents

▲ *Despite a threatening demeanor, silver dollars are placid fish that thrive on a diet of plants and seeds.*

▲ The male cobalt blue gourami has bright red barring on flanks and fins.

◀ The female has a more subdued colour pattern but still shines with iridescent blue.

Contents

▲ *A male orange sailfin molly, with a well-developed dorsal fin used in displays to females.*

▼ *The stunning silver arowana can reach 75cm in a large specialist community aquarium.*

184 -199

Oddballs

200 - 207

Choosing and buying fish

208

Picture credits and acknowledgements

Caring parents

▶ The cichlids are an extremely diverse family (Cichlidae), ranging in size from a couple of centimetres to almost a metre long, with considerable variations in shape and coloration. They are noted for their dietary specialisations – if something edible exists, a cichlid will have evolved to exploit it. Despite this variability, cichlids have one thing in common – they all look after their eggs and young. Some lay their eggs on a surface (substrate-brooders) and guard them and the resulting fry, others protect the eggs and/or larvae in the mouth(s) of one or both parents, usually the mother (mouthbrooders). This behaviour is fascinating but does have a downside – defending the brood often means attacking other fishes sharing the aquarium. Cichlids are found throughout the tropics in the Americas and Africa, plus three species in Asia (India/Sri Lanka), and are grouped here accordingly.

Price guide

★	Up to £3
★★	£3 – 10
★★★	£10 – 25
★★★★	£25 – 50
★★★★★	£50 +

FISH PROFILE

One of the earliest cichlids imported for the hobby, and still a great favourite – deservedly as it is colourful, relatively peaceful, and easy to keep.

WHAT size?
To 12.5cm, with males usually slightly larger than females.

WHAT does it eat?
An omnivore that will eat any foods of suitable size. Loves earthworms.

WHERE is it from?
Trinidad and northern Venezuela, in still or slow-moving waters.

WHAT does it cost?
★☆☆☆☆   ★★★☆☆
Usually cheap, though the occasional imports of wild fish are more expensive.

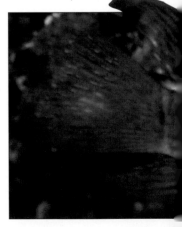

Blue acara

HOW do I sex it?
Males are supposedly larger with longer fins, but in practice the sexes are virtually indistinguishable except by the genital papillae when spawning.

WHAT kind of tank?
Best in a species tank, but can share with robust fishes in a large tank (120x40x40cm upwards).

WHAT minimum size tank?
90x30x30cm for a pair.

WHAT kind of water?
Tank-breds are unfussy as long as very acid water (pH less than 6) is avoided; wild fish are found in soft to moderately hard water with a pH of 6.8-7.5, depending on the location.

▲ *A juvenile blue acara showing the attractive iridescent patterns.*

▼ *Adult blue acaras have a very wide head, giving them a characteristic expression.*

HOW warm?
Again, not fussy: 23.5-27°C. The upper part of this range is best for wild fishes.

WHAT decor?
Rocks, clay flowerpots/pipes, weathered bogwood. Plants may be uprooted.

WHAT area of the tank?
Bottom to middle.

HOW many in one tank?
One or a pair, except if growing on unsexed juveniles. However, several adult females will live together peacefully if no male is present, and even 'pair' and lay eggs.

HOW does it behave?
Relatively peaceful, but aggressive (may attack – and bite – hands) when guarding fry!

WILL it breed in an aquarium?
Yes, readily, if both sexes are present.

Amphilophus citrinellus

Midas cichlid

FISH PROFILE

A splendid large cichlid. A single specimen in a tank of its own makes an excellent pet for any aquarist, but breeding is best left to those with experience in aggression management.

WHAT size?
Males to 34cm, females significantly smaller.

WHAT does it eat?
An omnivorous species that will eat any foods of suitable size, including small fishes.

WHERE is it from?
Chiefly the great lakes of Nicaragua, Central America.

WHAT does it cost?
★☆☆☆☆   ★★★☆☆
Practically nothing for juveniles (breeders often give them away) but a large adult suitable for showing commands a much higher price.

HOW do I sex it?
Males are larger, have longer fins, and are more aggressive. Adult males develop a nuchal hump.

WHAT kind of tank?
Species tank only.

WHAT minimum size tank?
90x45x45cm for a single adult, 120x45x45cm for a pair.

WHAT kind of water?
Moderately hard to very hard, pH7.5 or higher.

HOW warm?
23.5-27°C.

WHAT decor?
Rocks, weathered bogwood, clay pipes. Plants will be demolished.

WHAT area of the tank?
Bottom to middle levels.

HOW many in one tank?
One or a pair, except if growing on unsexed juveniles.

HOW does it behave?
Disgracefully! Males are extremely territorial and aggressive, both sexes dig, and equipment may be dislodged unless firmly siliconed in place.

WILL it breed in an aquarium?
Yes, but in a confined space males are often murderously aggressive towards females, even when young have hatched. A divider is an essential accessory. A pair is best obtained by growing on 5-6 juveniles.

▼ *This is a male of the yellow form of the Midas cichlid, with a well-developed nuchal hump.*

Apistogramma cacatuoides

Cockatoo dwarf cichlid

FISH PROFILE

Small, attractive and peaceful for a cichlid. Absolutely fascinating breeding behaviour.

WHAT size?
Males grow to 7cm, females only 2-2.5 cm.

WHAT does it eat?
In nature, small aquatic organisms; in captivity, small live or frozen live foods. Will also take some flake.

WHERE is it from?
The Peruvian part of the Amazon Basin.

WHAT does it cost?
★☆☆☆☆   ★★★☆☆
Moderately expensive from shops, often cheaper from breeders.

◀ *A male displays his vibrant fins.*

HOW do I sex it?
Males are much larger, with longer, more ornate finnage and brighter coloration. Full-grown males have very large mouths.

WHAT kind of tank?
Community tank or specialist aquarium.

WHAT minimum size tank?
60x30x30cm.

WHAT kind of water?
Ideally soft and slightly acid to slightly alkaline (pH6.0-7.5), but will breed even in harder water. Excellent quality required. Avoid strong currents.

◀ *The female is smaller and less colourful than the male.*

HOW warm?
26-27°C.

WHAT decor?
Fine gravel or sand, with plants and small flowerpot caves.

WHAT area of the tank?
Primarily near the bottom.

HOW many in one tank?
No limit provided each female has a 30cm-diameter territory of her own.

HOW does it behave?
Quite capable of defending a brood against much larger fish, but relies more on intimidation than injury.

WILL it breed in an aquarium?
Yes. Will breed in pairs, but the norm is for the male to have a harem of several females, each with her own territory within his. Breeding caves should have very small entrances and low ceilings. Brood care is normally carried out by the female(s) alone.

Astronolus ocellatus

Oscar

FISH PROFILE

Arguably the best-known and most popular large cichlid, noted for its character.

WHAT size?
Males and females to 26cm.

WHAT does it eat?
Omnivorous with strong piscivorous tendencies, even when young. Relishes small tankmates.

WHERE is it from?
Amazon drainage, South America.

WHAT does it cost?
★☆☆☆☆   ★★☆☆☆
Tank-bred youngsters are usually cheap, adults more expensive.

▼ *A large oscar is a real character and can soon recognise its owner.*

HOW do I sex it?
This is considered impossible except during spawning – females have a short, blunt genital papilla, while the male's is thinner and pointed.

WHAT kind of tank?
Single-species tank, optionally with a large armoured catfish (plec) as scavenger.

WHAT minimum size tank?
90x45x45cm for a single specimen, 120x45x45cm for a pair.

WHAT kind of water?
Ideally soft and slightly acid (essential for breeding), but thrives in any water.

HOW warm?
25-27°C.

WHAT decor?
Rocks, bogwood, large clay pots and/or pipes. The decor must be bedded on the bottom of the aquarium to prevent undermining. Live plants are vandalised, but plastic plants are appreciated as toys.

WHAT area of the tank?
Bottom to middle.

HOW many in one tank?
One or a pair when adult. A group of juveniles can be grown on together to get a pair. Females will live together peacefully when adult, males will not.

▼ *Oscars are available in several colour variants, including this tiger.*

HOW does it behave?
Usually badly! Apart from stormy courtship and eating tankmates, these fishes will move equipment and/or bury heaters and filter inlets with gravel. The tank should be 'Oscar-proofed' by siliconing equipment in place, off the bottom.

WILL it breed in an aquarium?
Yes, provided both sexes are present. Two females may 'pair' and spawn together in the absence of a male. Soft, acid water is needed to produce viable eggs.

▶ These are juveniles of the tiger (near right) and red (far right) colour forms.

"Cichlasoma" octofasciatum

Jack Dempsey

FISH PROFILE

A very easy and interesting cichlid to keep and breed. It has glorious colour and loads of character.

WHAT size?
Males grow to 17cm, females somewhat smaller.

WHAT does it eat?
Carnivorous/piscivorous, hence earthworms, shrimp, prawn, raw fish and carnivore pellets.

WHERE is it from?
Southern Mexico, Guatemala, and Honduras, in swamps and slow-moving rivers, as well as the sink-holes of the Yucatan.

WHAT does it cost?
★☆☆☆☆   ★★☆☆☆
Usually quite cheap.

HOW do I sex it?
Males are larger, with longer fins, and tend to lose their juvenile barring. Females retain their barring and may become very dark when breeding.

WHAT kind of tank?
Species tank.

WHAT minimum size tank?
90x40x40cm.

WHAT kind of water?
Good quality, moderately hard to very hard, pH7.5 or higher. Avoid strong currents.

HOW warm?
25-26°C.

WHAT decor?
Rocks and bogwood. Will dig up plants.

WHAT area of the tank?
Primarily near the bottom.

HOW many in one tank?
One or a pair.

HOW does it behave?
Rather territorial, especially when breeding. Best not kept with other fish.

WILL it breed in an aquarium?
Yes. Care of the fry lasts only 10-14 days, after which they may be eaten as the pair prepare to spawn again. Any fry required for rearing should be removed about a week after they become free swimming.

▲ This female Jack Dempsey is darker than normal.

▶ A male with typical coloration and long fins. The juvenile barring is still visible towards the tail.

Crenicichla compressiceps

FISH PROFILE

A delightful but difficult little pike cichlid, a challenge even for the cichlid expert.

▲ *A pair of* Crenicichla compressiceps, *with the larger male in front.*

WHAT size?
Males to around 7cm, females smaller.

WHAT does it eat?
In nature, mainly aquatic invertebrates and fish fry, in captivity they do best on similar live foods.

WHERE is it from?
Rio Tocantins drainage, Brazil.

WHAT does it cost?
★★★☆☆
Quite expensive, as most stocks are wild adults. Tank-breds are rare and command a good price too.

HOW do I sex it?
Males are larger and often more boldly patterned than females.

WHAT kind of tank?
Species tank.

WHAT minimum size tank?
90x30x30cm for a pair.

WHAT kind of water?
Very soft and slightly acid (pH 6-6.5), well-oxygenated, and very good quality.

HOW warm?
25-28°C.

WHAT decor?
The natural habitat is usually rocky, but bogwood can be included as well. Plants are not harmed.

WHAT area of the tank?
Bottom to middle levels.

HOW many in one tank?
One pair, or a small group in a very large tank (180x40x40cm minimum for a group of 5-6).

HOW does it behave?
Unfortunately, intraspecific aggression is a problem with single pairs, even when breeding. This can sometimes be averted by adding some tetras and/or small catfishes as a distraction, or keeping two pairs separated by a clear divider in a larger tank (120cm minimum length) so that aggression is directed against the other pair instead of the partner.

WILL it breed in an aquarium?
Yes, if the aggression problem can be solved.

Cryptoheros nigrofasciatus

Convict cichlid

FISH PROFILE

One of the most commonplace and popular cichlids in the hobby, ideal for the beginner to keep and breed. As well as the natural striped form, there is a cultivated albino variety.

WHAT size?
Males to around 7.5cm, females a lot smaller.

WHAT does it eat?
Naturally omnivorous, with a large algae component, but more carnivorous in captivity. May eat small tankmates.

WHERE is it from?
Central America, from Guatemala to Panama.

WHAT does it cost?
★☆☆☆☆   ★★☆☆☆
Juveniles are cheap or free from breeders, tank-bred adults inexpensive; wild fish are scarcely ever seen so no price information available.

HOW do I sex it?
Females are smaller and have metallic orange in the dorsal, and sometimes on the belly. Size is the only criterion in the albino form.

WHAT kind of tank?
Species tank or community of small Central American cichlids. NOT suitable for a general community, though often sold as such.

WHAT minimum size tank?
60x40x40cm for a single pair, 120x40x40cm if sharing.

WHAT kind of water?
Moderately hard to very hard, pH7.5 or higher, but not critical as long as very acid (less than pH6) conditions are avoided.

HOW warm?
23.5-27°C.

WHAT decor?
Rocks, weathered bogwood and/or clay flowerpots. Plants are likely to be uprooted unless grown in pots or between rocks.

WHAT area of the tank?
Bottom.

HOW many in one tank?
Preferably no more than one pair per tank.

HOW does it behave?
In the wild this species has to battle vigorously for territory, so it tends to be very competitive in the aquarium as well.

WILL it breed in an aquarium?
A cave-breeding substrate-spawner. Very easy to breed and the fish make excellent parents.

◀ *The normal, striped form of the convict cichlid.*

▼ *The albino form will pair readily with the normal form.*

Geophagus steindachneri

Red-hump eartheater

FISH PROFILE

Although *Geophagus* are something of a minority interest, this species has achieved more general popularity, perhaps because of its ease of maintenance and breeding.

WHAT size?
Males rarely more than 12cm, females smaller.

WHAT does it eat?
An omnivorous bottom-sifting species, which should have some vegetable food in the diet.

WHERE is it from?
The Rio Magdalena drainage in Colombia.

WHAT does it cost?
★★☆☆☆
Unusually, this species was never particularly expensive, even when first imported. Sometimes sold as *G. pellegrini* (a rarely seen, related species) at inflated prices.

HOW do I sex it?
Adult males are larger and more colourful and have a red-brown hump, females are plain olive-beige.

WHAT kind of tank?
Species tank or community of similar-sized fishes.

WHAT minimum size tank?
90x40x40cm for a single pair, 120x40x40cm for a larger group or community.

WHAT kind of water?
Ideally slightly hard and alkaline (pH7.2-7.8), but unfussy.

HOW warm?
23.5-27°C.

WHAT decor?
Rocks, weathered bogwood, sandy or fine gravel substrate. Plants should be grown in pots or between stones to prevent uprooting during sifting.

WHAT area of the tank?
Bottom to middle levels.

HOW many in one tank?
Can be kept as a pair, a male with two or more females, or a group of both sexes. If several males are kept they develop huge humps, apparently stimulated by competition.

HOW does it behave?
Rather peaceful among themselves and towards other fishes.

WILL it breed in an aquarium?
Yes, with ease. An advanced maternal mouthbrooder with a brooding period of around two weeks. The male plays no part in brood care.

▼ *The male (left) has a red hump, absent in the female.*

Microgeophagus ramirezi

Ram, butterfly dwarf cichlid

A delightful dwarf cichlid, kept by many aquarists, but rarely with much success because of poor-quality stock and ignorance of its rather stringent requirements.

◀ *A pair of rams (male right).*

WHAT size?
Males and females up to 6.5cm.

WHAT does it eat?
In nature, mainly aquatic invertebrates. Live and/or frozen live foods should be the main diet in captivity.

WHERE is it from?
Pools and streams in the Orinoco drainage in Colombia and Venezuela.

WHAT does it cost?
★☆☆☆☆   ★★☆☆☆
Most stock is cheap, mass-produced in the Far East. Home-bred stock is a little dearer but well worth the extra.

HOW do I sex it?
Females have a mauve-pink area on the lower flank.

WHAT kind of tank?
General community; species tank; South American dwarf cichlid community.

WHAT minimum size tank?
60x30x30cm for a pair, 90x40x40cm community.

WHAT kind of water?
Very soft, slightly acid water (pH6-6.5) is required for long-term survival and breeding. The water should be of very good quality. Avoid strong currents.

HOW warm?
25-28°C.

WHAT decor?
A well-planted tank with bogwood, and caves (clay flowerpots) concealed among the other decor.

WHAT area of the tank?
Mainly bottom.

HOW many in one tank?
Several pairs can be kept in larger tanks. Allow about 40cm of tank length per pair, as their exclusive territory (not shared with other bottom-dwelling cichlids).

HOW does it behave?
A very peaceful cichlid, even when breeding.

WILL it breed in an aquarium?
Yes, but this is rarely achieved because of the problems of poor stock and incorrect maintenance.

Parachromis managuensis

Jaguar cichlid, mannie

FISH PROFILE

A real character, which, kept singly, makes an excellent pet, but is also noted for long-term 'happy marriages'.

WHAT size?
Males to 55cm, females smaller; usually only half this size in captivity.

WHAT does it eat?
The natural diet is fish, but it will also take carnivore pellets, shrimps, prawns, earthworms.

WHERE is it from?
Originally probably restricted to the Nicaraguan lakes, but introduced as a food fish elsewhere in Central America.

WHAT does it cost?
★☆☆☆☆   ★★☆☆☆
Breeders often give youngsters away; even a large adult or breeding pair is usually quite cheap.

▼ *The female jaguar cichlid is lighter-coloured than the male.*

HOW do I sex it?
Adult males dark mottled all over, females paler with a dark longitudinal band. Juveniles unsexable.

WHAT kind of tank?
Species tank.

WHAT minimum size tank?
90x45x45cm for a single adult, 120x45x45cm for a pair.

WHAT kind of water?
Moderately hard to very hard, pH7.5 or higher.

HOW warm?
23.5-27°C.

WHAT decor?
Rocks, weathered bogwood, clay pots and/or pipes, bedded on the tank bottom to avoid undermining. Plants will be uprooted.

WHAT area of the tank?
Bottom to middle levels.

HOW many in one tank?
One or a pair, except when growing on unsexable youngsters.

HOW does it behave?
Like any large piscivorous cichlid, this fish will eat small tankmates and defend its territory with considerable vigour, hence the need for a species tank. But pairs are noted for living in harmony for years. Digs enthusiastically.

WILL it breed in an aquarium?
Yes, readily. Broods are huge, and culling is essential. The parents will see to this if the fry are left with them too long.

Pterophyllum scalare

Angel

FISH PROFILE

Probably the most popular of all cichlids, but so unusual in shape that many people don't realise it's a cichlid at all. Available in numerous man-made forms, varying in both colour and finnage.

WHAT size?
Males and females to around 13cm long and rather more deep, but usually smaller.

WHAT does it eat?
In nature, mainly aquatic invertebrates; in captivity they will take any omnivore or carnivore foods.

WHERE is it from?
Amazon drainage, South America.

WHAT does it cost?
★☆☆☆☆   ★★★☆☆
Price varies from very cheap home-bred youngsters to fairly expensive wild adults and new cultivated forms.

▶ Angels are available in colour forms, some of which are shown on these pages.

▶ Altum angels (Pt. altum) are rare, expensive and very difficult to keep.

HOW do I sex it?

Although many people claim to be able to detect external differences, they are realistically sexable only by the shape of the genital papilla during spawning – male pointed, female blunt. Buy a group to obtain a pair.

WHAT kind of tank?

General community; species tank.

WHAT minimum size tank?

60x40x40cm for a pair, 90x40x40cm community.

WHAT kind of water?

Tank-bred strains thrive in any water chemistry, but soft, slightly acid (pH6-6.5) water required for wild fish and breeding. Avoid strong filter currents.

HOW warm?

25-28°C.

WHAT decor?

Ideally a well-planted tank with bogwood, but not critical for tank-bred strains.

WHAT area of the tank?

Middle to top.

HOW many in one tank?

Shoals in nature, so no limit given adequate space.

HOW does it behave?

A very peaceful cichlid even when breeding, but will sometimes eat very small tankmates.

WILL it breed in an aquarium?

Yes, but most tank-breds eat their brood, so artificial hatching may be needed. Two females will 'pair' and spawn together if no male is present.

◀ *There are also different types of finnage: 'lace' above (on a wild-caught specimen), and normal below.*

23

Symphysodon aequifasciatus

Discus, pompadour

FISH PROFILE

A cult fish, available in numerous man-made colour varieties. Although this is an easy, hardy fish if kept properly, it is all too frequently portrayed as requiring bare tanks, dangerously high temperatures, and special, usually unsuitable, diets. The result is that many discus are highly stressed, short-lived, neurotic wrecks.

WHAT size?
Males and females to around 15cm in diameter.

WHAT does it eat?
In nature, mainly aquatic invertebrates; in captivity, any omnivore/carnivore foods, including flake.

WHERE is it from?
Amazon drainage, South America.

WHAT does it cost?
★★☆☆☆   ★★★★★
Price varies from fairly cheap for youngsters of established strains to ridiculous for some wild adults and new cultivated forms.

HOW do I sex it?
Sexable only by the shape of the genital papilla during spawning – male pointed, female blunt.

WHAT kind of tank?
General community; species tank.

WHAT minimum size tank?
60x30x45cm for a pair, 90x30x45cm community.

WHAT kind of water?
Tank-bred strains thrive in any water chemistry, but soft, slightly acid (pH6-6.5) water required for wild fish and breeding. Avoid strong filter currents.

HOW warm?
25-28°C.

WHAT decor?
Ideally bogwood and established, tall plants to provide shade.

WHAT area of the tank?
Middle to top levels.

HOW many in one tank?
Shoals in nature, so no limit given adequate space, and best kept in groups.

▶ Discus fry feed on a special parental skin secretion.

▶ One of many man-made red varieties.

HOW does it behave?

Adults are peaceful, even when breeding. Youngsters may bully (to death) the smallest if no adult is present to keep them in order. Problems with shyness and fussy feeding are normally indicative of incorrect maintenance.

WILL it breed in an aquarium?

Yes. The fry feed initially on a special secretion produced by the parents, and must be left with them for this reason.

Selective breeding and crossing have created innumerable discus variants very different from the original wild fish.

Thorichthys meeki

Firemouth

A staple of the cichlid hobby, famed for its magnificent frontal threat display. The gill covers bear an eye-like spot, and when expanded in threat make the fish look much larger than it really is.

WHAT size?
Male and females to 12cm, usually smaller.

WHAT does it eat?
A carnivore that will eat any suitable foods, including small tankmates.

WHERE is it from?
Mainly Mexico, extending into Belize and Guatemala.

WHAT does it cost?
★☆☆☆☆   ★★★☆☆

Juveniles are cheap, tank-bred adults relatively inexpensive. Wild fish are rarely seen and more expensive.

▲ *An adult male firemouth moves forward to investigate a threat.*

▲ *The red on the lower part of the head gives the firemouth its name.*

HOW do I sex it?
Males have slightly longer finnage, but it is best to grow on a group of youngsters to get a pair.

WHAT kind of tank?
Species tank or community of small Central American cichlids.

WHAT minimum size tank?
75x30x30cm for a single pair, 120x40x40cm if sharing.

WHAT kind of water?
Moderately hard to very hard, pH7.5 or higher.

HOW warm?
23.5-27°C.

WHAT decor?
Rocks, weathered bogwood, clay flowerpots. Plants can be grown in pots or between rocks to avoid accidental uprooting.

WHAT area of the tank?
Bottom to middle levels.

HOW many in one tank?
Ideally keep two or more pairs to see the display. Allow 60cm of tank length per pair.

HOW does it behave?
Quite peaceful, the display is usually just a warning. But not a fish for the general community, though often sold as such – too boisterous and likely to eat small fishes.

WILL it breed in an aquarium?
Quite easy to breed. A substrate-spawner with a preference for the walls of caves or overhangs as spawning sites.

Vieja synspila

Synspilum or quetzal cichlid

FISH PROFILE

One of a group of large, usually colourful, omnivorous cichlids that are very popular with hobbyists, although not as inclined to 'character' as the large carnivores.

WHAT size?
Males and females to around 26cm.

WHAT does it eat?
Will take almost any food, but a reasonable vegetable component is important.

WHERE is it from?
Southern Mexico, Guatemala, and Belize.

WHAT does it cost?
★☆☆☆☆ ★★★☆☆
Juveniles are cheap (or free from breeders), while a large breeding pair or show specimen commands a higher price.

HOW do I sex it?
No sexual differences visible except at spawning time, when the female has a larger, blunter genital papilla. Both sexes may develop a nuchal hump when full-grown, with that of the male sometimes larger.

WHAT kind of tank?
Species tank when full-grown, juveniles and young pairs (up to about 10cm) can be kept with other robust fishes in large tanks (120cm upwards).

WHAT minimum size tank?
90x45x45cm for a single adult, 120x45x45cm for a full-grown pair.

WHAT kind of water?
Hard and alkaline, pH 7.5 or higher.

HOW warm?
23.5-27°C.

WHAT decor?
Rocks, weathered bogwood, clay pipes. Soft-leaved plants are likely to be browsed, and any plants uprooted.

WHAT area of the tank?
Bottom to middle.

HOW many in one tank?
One or a pair, except when growing on unsexed juveniles to obtain a pair.

HOW does it behave?
Remarkably peaceful and non-destructive for a cichlid this size, but no fish with a natural territory 240cm or more in diameter can be expected to be angelic in a confined space.

WILL it breed in an aquarium?
Yes, and it is unusual for there to be any (serious) conflict between the sexes. Will hybridise with other *Vieja* to produce viable fry, so shouldn't be mixed with them.

▶ A non-breeding female synspilum. The colours intensify considerably at spawning time.

Altolamprologus compressiceps

FISH PROFILE

A very attractive, small, rock-dwelling cichlid with several geographical colour variants. It is regarded as difficult and a fish for the cichlid specialist because of its tendency to nervousness and stringent requirements as regards water chemistry and quality. Breeding is an even greater challenge.

WHAT size?
Males up to 13cm, females up to 8.5cm, often smaller.

WHAT does it eat?
In nature, fish fry and aquatic invertebrates. Best fed on live and frozen foods, but will take flake.

WHERE is it from?
Lake Tanganyika, East Africa.

WHAT does it cost?
★★☆☆   ★★★★☆
Wild fish are expensive. Tank-breds are scarce and command high prices.

HOW do I sex it?
Males are far larger than females.

WHAT kind of tank?
Species aquarium or Tanganyika cichlid community.

WHAT minimum size tank?
60x30x45cm for a pair or trio in a species tank.

WHAT kind of water?
Moderately to very hard, alkaline (pH8+), well-oxygenated, and minimal nitrogenous compounds.

HOW warm?
25-27°C.

WHAT decor?
Copious rockwork with plenty of small vertical crevices.

WHAT area of the tank?
Bottom to middle levels.

HOW many in one tank?
Allow at least 45cm of tank length per pair.

HOW does it behave?
Rather timid and peaceful, but fierce in territorial defence when breeding.

WILL it breed in an aquarium?
Yes, but spawning is difficult to achieve, and the fry are often eaten by the male. He plays no part in fry care and may spawn with multiple females in succession.

The predatory nature of A. compressiceps is apparent from the form of the mouth.

Aulonocara jacobfreibergi

Malawi butterfly

FISH PROFILE

This fish combines colour with an elegance of form not seen in many Malawi cichlids. Unfortunately, it is often kept with inappropriate tankmates where it isn't seen at its best.

WHAT size?
Males and females up to about 8.5cm.

WHAT does it eat?
The natural diet is aquatic invertebrates, so best fed frozen foods. Too much dried food may cause 'Malawi bloat'.

WHERE is it from?
Lake Malawi, East Africa.

WHAT does it cost?
★★☆☆☆   ★★★☆☆
Tank-bred youngsters are relatively cheap, wild adults more expensive.

HOW do I sex it?
Males are colourful, females not.

WHAT kind of tank?
Malawi community with sand-dwellers or open-water species, NOT rock-dwellers.

WHAT minimum size tank?
90x30x45cm.

WHAT kind of water?
Moderately hard and alkaline (pH7.5+), well-oxygenated, and minimal nitrogenous compounds.

HOW warm?
25-26°C.

WHAT decor?
Open sand at the front, large rock caves at the rear. In nature, it lives in and around large underwater caves opening onto a sandy bottom.

WHAT area of the tank?
Bottom-dweller.

HOW many in one tank?
No limits within normal stocking rules, but allow about 45cm of tank length per male.

HOW does it behave?
A rather peaceful cichlid.

WILL it breed in an aquarium?
Like most maternal mouthbrooders, this fish is easy to breed if kept correctly. Unfortunately, many are kept with the aggressive, rock dwelling Malawi mbuna (see page 38), and do not thrive, let alone breed. Do not mix with other *Aulonocara* species or hybridisation may occur.

▼ *A male Malawi butterfly. Females lack the gorgeous colours seen here.*

29

Copadichromis borleyi

Borleyi

FISH PROFILE

One of the open-water, zoo-plankton-feeding group of Malawi cichlid species known as 'utaka', both locally and in the hobby. A number of geographical variants are known, probably the most popular being the 'Kadango' seen here.

▶ *Utaka are not tied to any particular biotope, but this species is usually found close to rocky shore so a rocky background (real or artificial) is preferable.*

WHAT size?
Males to about 14cm, females to 11cm.

WHAT does it eat?
The natural diet is aquatic invertebrates, so best fed live and/or frozen foods. Will also take chopped shrimp/prawn. Too much dried food may cause 'Malawi bloat'.

WHERE is it from?
Inshore waters all around Lake Malawi, East Africa.

WHAT does it cost?
★★☆☆☆   ★★★☆☆
Tank-bred youngsters are relatively cheap, wild adults more expensive but rarely available.

HOW do I sex it?
Males are colourful, females are plain silvery, brownish, or yellowish, depending on the variant. Females of the Kadango form have red-orange unpaired fins.

WHAT kind of tank?
Malawi community with sand-dwellers and other open-water species, NOT mbuna.

WHAT minimum size tank?
120x30x45cm.

WHAT kind of water?
Moderately hard and alkaline (pH 7.5 or higher), well-oxygenated, and minimal nitrogenous compounds.

HOW warm?
25-27°C.

WHAT decor?
Plenty of swimming space is the main requirement, but rocks and/or plants can be included for aesthetic reasons.

WHAT area of the tank?
Middle to upper levels; bottom when spawning.

HOW many in one tank?
A shoaling fish, so no limits within normal stocking rules.

HOW does it behave?
Rather peaceful, as is to be expected in shoaling species.

WILL it breed in an aquarium?
Like almost all Malawi cichlids, this is a maternal mouthbrooder and will breed readily if correctly maintained.

Cyphotilapia frontosa

Frontosa

FISH PROFILE

Frontosas are attractive and justifiably popular, but should come with a health warning: 'This fish grows big and eats tankmates.'

WHAT size?
Males up to 21cm, females up to 17cm.

WHAT does it eat?
A piscivorous species whose diet should include raw fish, as well as shrimp, prawn, earthworms and carnivore pellets. Feed at dawn and dusk, when it feeds in nature.

WHERE is it from?
Lake Tanganyika, East Africa.

WHAT does it cost?
★★★☆☆   ★★★★☆
Expensive – wild fish cost a lot to capture and transport, and demand for tank-breds outstrips supply.

HOW do I sex it?
Males are larger, have longer fins and larger humps. No colour differences.

WHAT kind of tank?
Species tank. Best in groups or sharing with other large, relatively peaceful Tanganyikan or Malawi cichlids.

WHAT minimum size tank?
120x35x45cm.

WHAT kind of water?
Hard, alkaline (pH 8+), well-oxygenated, and minimal nitrogenous compounds.

HOW warm?
23.5-26°C.

WHAT decor?
Open sand/gravel with scattered large rocks and caves (clay pipes are ideal).

WHAT area of the tank?
Strictly a bottom-dweller.

HOW many in one tank?
No limit within normal stocking rules.

HOW does it behave?
Adults are peaceful and rather inactive (in line with their natural feeding cycle), but will eat any tankmates that will fit into their mouths.

WILL it breed in an aquarium?
Yes. The species is a maternal mouthbrooder, and the female should be removed to a separate tank to release her fry, which will otherwise be eaten immediately by the other frontosas!

▼ *Male frontosas have bigger humps than females.*

Cyprichromis sp. 'Leptosoma jumbo'

Leptosoma jumbo

One of the popular 'cypricichlids' from Lake Tanganyika. These peaceful shoaling fishes live off the bottom and are valuable for filling the often empty upper levels of Tanganyikan communities. The name of this as yet undescribed species reflects its similarity to the smaller *C. leptosoma.*

WHAT size?
Males and females to 10.5cm.

WHAT does it eat?
Feeds on zooplankton in open water in the wild. Reluctant to follow sinking foods to the bottom, but will eat most carnivore/omnivore foods in the aquarium, including flake.

WHERE is it from?
Rocky shoreline in southern Lake Tanganyika, East Africa.

WHAT does it cost?
★★☆☆☆   ★★★☆☆
Wild fish are quite expensive. Tank-breds are quite scarce and command a good price.

▲ *These active, streamlined fish have large eyes and long pectoral fins.*

HOW do I sex it?
Males are much more colourful.

WHAT kind of tank?
Species tank, or upper levels of a community of small, bottom-dwelling Tanganyikan cichlids.

WHAT minimum size tank?
90x45x45cm.

WHAT kind of water?
Hard, alkaline (pH8+), well-oxygenated, and minimal nitrogenous compounds.

HOW warm?
24-27°C.

WHAT decor?
Rocky background (internal or external) extending up to the surface, with open water in front. Bottom decor to suit any fishes living there.

▲ *A male leptosoma jumbo, a striking fish that will bring constant movement to the aquarium. Best kept in shoals.*

WHAT area of the tank?
Upper levels, but may – as in nature – descend to the substrate at night.

HOW many in one tank?
No maximum within normal stocking rules, but a minimum shoal of six is recommended.

HOW does it behave?
Very peaceful for a cichlid, though males may squabble.

WILL it breed in an aquarium?
Yes, it is a maternal mouthbrooder and quite easy to breed, but the fry can be tricky to feed.

Cyrtocara moorii

Malawi blue dolphin cichlid

FISH PROFILE

In nature, this species follows large sand-sifting cichlids, feeding on any 'fallout', and males defend their host (as a mobile feeding territory) against other *moorii* males, though females are welcome to share!

WHAT size?
Males up to 17.5cm, females slightly smaller.

WHAT does it eat?
In nature, mainly aquatic invertebrates; in captivity, best fed frozen foods. Too much dry food may cause 'Malawi bloat'.

WHERE is it from?
Lake Malawi, East Africa.

WHAT does it cost?
★★☆☆☆   ★★★☆☆
Tank-bred youngsters are fairly cheap, wild adults more expensive.

HOW do I sex it?
Males are usually larger, but there are no obvious sexual differences.

WHAT kind of tank?
Malawi community with other sand-dwellers or open-water species, but NOT with rock-dwellers.

WHAT minimum size tank?
120x30x45cm.

WHAT kind of water?
Moderately hard, alkaline (pH 7.5+), well-oxygenated, and minimal nitrogenous compounds.

HOW warm?
25-27°C.

WHAT decor?
Open sand or fine gravel with *Vallisneria* spp. and occasional rocks.

WHAT area of the tank?
Bottom-dweller.

HOW many in one tank?
No more than one male, except in very large tanks. As many females as desired.

HOW does it behave?
Very peaceful for its size, even when breeding.

WILL it breed in an aquarium?
Yes, this species is a maternal mouthbrooder and easy to breed if kept correctly. Unfortunately, many individuals spend miserable lives in tanks filled with rocks and rock-dwelling Malawi mbuna (see page 38), which are far more aggressive; such Malawi blue dolphin cichlids rarely breed.

▼ *The common name of this species relates to the dolphin-like head profile.*

33

Eretmodus cyanostictus

FISH PROFILE

One of the Lake Tanganyika goby cichlids – strange little fishes that have reduced swimbladders, an adaptation to living on rocks in the surf zone. Fascinating but difficult to keep.

Goby cichlids are also known as 'Tanganyika clowns' because of their comical appearance.

WHAT size?
Males up to 8cm, females about 6.5cm.

WHAT does it eat?
Scrapes algae from rocks and probably eats aquatic invertebrates living in this biocover. The aquarium diet should have a high vegetable component.

WHERE is it from?
Lake Tanganyika, East Africa.

WHAT does it cost?
★★★☆☆
Wild fish are quite expensive; tank-breds are very rare.

▲ *Small teeth ideal for rasping algae.*

HOW do I sex it?
No visible differences apart from size (males are larger).

WHAT kind of tank?
Species tank, or community of small Tanganyikan rock-dwellers.

WHAT minimum size tank?
120cm, and ideally at least 35cm wide/deep.

WHAT kind of water?
Hard, alkaline (pH 8+), very highly oxygenated, and minimal nitrogenous compounds.

HOW warm?
25-27°C.

WHAT decor?
Large amounts of rockwork, ideally extending up into the current from the filter return. Fine sand substrate – there are indications that the fish may deliberately consume sand.

WHAT area of the tank?
Upper surfaces of rocks at any level.

HOW many in one tank?
One pair, or a small group (allow 25-30cm of tank length per fish).

HOW does it behave?
Quite aggressive among themselves, hence the need for space.

WILL it breed in an aquarium?
Rarely achieved, chiefly because of incompatibility problems when trying to pair off (unsexable) wild adults. The best chance is offered by a group in a huge tank, so they can choose their own partners. The species is a biparental mouthbrooder in which the parents take turns to brood.

Hemichromis lifallili

Lifallili

FISH PROFILE

This species is very similar in appearance to the jewel cichlid, *H. guttatus*, but more suitable for the aquarium because it is less aggressive.

WHAT size?
Males and females up to 8.5cm.

WHAT does it eat?
In nature, aquatic invertebrates and fish fry; in the aquarium, any suitably sized carnivore foods.

WHERE is it from?
Mainly forest streams in central Africa.

WHAT does it cost?
★★☆☆☆ ★★★☆☆
Moderately expensive. Ideally, buy from a trustworthy specialist cichlid dealer, as it appears that in some quarters *H. guttatus* is being sold as this species, deliberately or through mistaken identity.

HOW do I sex it?
Sexing is virtually impossible. Look for two adults defending a territory together, or buy half a dozen youngsters.

WHAT kind of tank?
Species tank, perhaps with small armoured catfishes.

WHAT minimum size tank?
90x30x30cm for a pair.

WHAT kind of water?
Ideally soft and slightly acid (pH6-6.5). Will thrive in hard water but breeding may prove elusive.

HOW warm?
24.5-27°C.

WHAT decor?
A well-planted tank with bogwood and caves, and smooth stones (spawning sites) among the plants.

WHAT area of the tank?
Bottom to lower middle.

HOW many in one tank?
One pair (plus family).

HOW does it behave?
Hemichromis are predators that live solitarily (to avoid competition for prey), except when breeding. They thus tend to be very territorial, including towards potential partners, except when almost ready to spawn. This species is less aggressive than most, but still requires plenty of space so that the pair can avoid each other when not breeding.

WILL it breed in an aquarium?
Yes, assuming a compatible pair can be achieved and the water chemistry is correct. The species is an open-brooding substrate-spawner.

◀ A pair of *Hemichromis lifallili (male below)*.

Iodotropheus sprengerae

Rusty cichlid

Not one of the most colourful of the rock-dwelling cichlids (mbuna) of Lake Malawi, but less aggressive than most, so ideal for the smaller mbuna community aquarium.

▶ *A male rusty cichlid, showing some eggspots. The rows of small rasping teeth are clearly visible.*

WHAT size?
Males to around 8cm, females very slightly smaller.

WHAT does it eat?
This species is omnivorous and feeds on both algae and invertebrates in the wild. It will eat almost any food offered, but include plenty of vegetable matter and avoid more than minimal amounts of dried foods, which can lead to fatal 'Malawi bloat'.

WHERE is it from?
Small rocky islands and reefs in the south of Lake Malawi, East Africa.

WHAT does it cost?
★☆☆☆☆   ★★★☆☆
Wild adults are fairly expensive and rarely seen nowadays. Most of the available stock is hobbyist-bred and cheaper.

HOW do I sex it?
The sexes are very similar. Look for more black in the fins and more eggspots in males.

WHAT kind of tank?
Mbuna-only community.

WHAT minimum size tank?
90x40x40cm, but the larger the better.

WHAT kind of water?
Moderately hard, alkaline (pH 7.5+), well-oxygenated, and minimal nitrogenous compounds.

HOW warm?
25-27°C.

WHAT decor?
Huge amounts of rockwork in the aquarium, arranged to provide numerous caves.

WHAT area of the tank?
Any level to which the rockwork extends.

HOW many in one tank?
Only one male (except in very large tanks), but several females if desired.

HOW does it behave?
Relatively peaceful compared to many mbuna, and males rarely harass females.

WILL it breed in an aquarium?
A maternal mouthbrooder that, given correct maintenance, will breed without any special additional treatment. Females can be left to brood in the community if their tankmates are similarly peaceful, or be removed to a brooding tank (where the fry are easier to catch).

Julidochromis transcriptus

FISH PROFILE

The 'Julies' are all popular with aquarists because of their attractive appearance and interesting behaviour. Their ability to swim backwards, or on their sides/upside-down with their bellies towards the nearest rock, is fascinating to watch. This species is one of the smallest and easiest to keep and breed.

WHAT size?
Males to 7cm, females smaller.

WHAT does it eat?
In nature, aquatic invertebrates. Live and frozen foods are best in the aquarium, though these fishes will take prepared foods too.

WHERE is it from?
Rocky coastline in various parts of Lake Tanganyika.

WHAT does it cost?
★★☆☆☆
★★★☆☆
Wild fish are fairly expensive; tank-breds are not common enough to be cheap.

HOW do I sex it?
Apart from the size difference, in adult males the genital papilla is usually permanently visible.

WHAT kind of tank?
Species tank, or community of small Tanganyikan rock-dwellers.

WHAT minimum size tank?
60x30x30cm for a pair living alone.

WHAT kind of water?
Moderately hard to very hard, alkaline (pH 8+), well-oxygenated, minimal nitrogenous compounds, no strong currents.

HOW warm?
25-27°C.

WHAT decor?
Plenty of rockwork providing small caves and crevices.

WHAT area of the tank?
Mainly near the bottom, but anywhere there are rocks.

HOW many in one tank?
One pair unless the tank is huge.

HOW does it behave?
Quite aggressive among themselves, but generally ignore other fishes.

WILL it breed in an aquarium?
A cave-breeding substrate-spawner. Breeding any Julie is considered an achievement. Avoid disturbing breeding pairs, as this may result in 'divorce', possibly with the loss of one partner.

▼ Julidochromis transcriptus *varies geographically – this is the 'Kelimi' form.*

Labeotropheus trewavasae

Trewavas's mbuna

FISH PROFILE

One of the mbuna, the local name for the colourful rock dwellers of Lake Malawi. This species is noted for its astonishing 'nose', as well as its colour morphs and relatively peaceful behaviour.

WHAT size?
Males up to 12.5cm, females a little smaller.

WHAT does it eat?
In nature it feeds on the 'Aufwuchs' (thick algae) covering the rocks, as well as any invertebrates it contains. In the aquarium it requires an omnivore diet with plenty of vegetable matter. Avoid large amounts of dried foods, which can lead to the lethal illness 'Malawi bloat'.

WHERE is it from?
Lake Malawi, East Africa.

WHAT does it cost?
★☆☆☆☆   ★★★☆☆
Prices range from cheap for tank-bred youngsters to fairly expensive for wild adults.

HOW do I sex it?
The sexes are differently coloured. (There are many colour forms and the patterns and colours vary between them.)

WHAT kind of tank?
Mbuna-only community aquarium.

WHAT minimum size tank?
90x30x45cm, but larger is better.

WHAT kind of water?
Moderately hard, alkaline (pH7.5+), well-oxygenated, and minimal nitrogenous compounds.

HOW warm?
25-27°C.

WHAT decor?
Vast amounts of rockwork providing numerous caves.

WHAT area of the tank?
Anywhere there are rocks and food. Less bottom-orientated than many mbuna.

HOW many in one tank?
No more than one male, except in very large tanks. One or several females.

HOW does it behave?
Relatively peaceful for an mbuna, and males rarely harass females.

WILL it breed in an aquarium?
Yes, it is a maternal mouthbrooder that is easy to breed if kept correctly. Females can be allowed to brood and release their fry in the community, but while this is fun to watch, the fry are easier to catch in a separate brooding tank!

▶ A male 'red top' Labeotropheus trewavasae. Many males have a blue dorsal fin.

Lamprologus ocellatus

FISH PROFILE

A Tanganyikan shell dweller, one of the tiniest cichlids known, and ideal for those with minimal space, as a pair can be kept in a small tank on a work surface. However, size isn't everything – this fish will attack a human hand in defence of its young!

L. ocellatus is tiny, but courageous in defence of its fry.

WHAT size?
Males up to 2.5cm, but females rarely exceed 2cm.

WHAT does it eat?
Aquatic invertebrates in the wild; best fed on small live/frozen live foods in captivity, but will take most small carnivore foods.

WHERE is it from?
Lake Tanganyika, East Africa.

WHAT does it cost?
★★☆☆☆   ★★★☆☆
Wild fish are quite expensive; tank-breds – if available – are cheaper.

HOW do I sex it?
No colour differences. Males are larger.

WHAT kind of tank?
Species tank, or community of small Tanganyikan cichlids.

WHAT minimum size tank?
45x30x30cm for a pair by themselves.

WHAT kind of water?
Hard, alkaline (pH 8+), well-oxygenated, minimal nitrogenous compounds.

HOW warm?
25-27°C.

WHAT decor?
Open sand with spiral shells – those of the French edible snail are ideal. The sand must be fine and at least 5cm deep so that the fishes can bury their shells.

WHAT area of the tank?
Exclusively a bottom-dweller.

HOW many in one tank?
No limit given adequate space, but allow 45cm of tank length per male.

HOW does it behave?
Quite aggressive, but not big enough to do much harm to anything other than each other.

WILL it breed in an aquarium?
Yes, this substrate-spawner breeds in pairs or harems of two to five females. Each female has her own shell in which she spawns and guards her young. A joy to watch!

Metriaclima zebra

Zebra cichlid

FISH PROFILE

One of the first mbuna (Lake Malawi rock-dwellers) imported. It is still one of the most popular on account of the stunning blue-and-black striping of the males and attractive orange-blotch coloration of some females.

WHAT size?
Males up to 10.5cm, females slightly smaller.

WHAT does it eat?
In nature, the biocover (thick algae containing invertebrates) on the rocks. In the aquarium provide an omnivore diet with plenty of vegetable matter and minimal amounts of dried foods (which can lead to fatal 'Malawi bloat').

WHERE is it from?
Lake Malawi, East Africa.

WHAT does it cost?
★☆☆☆☆   ★★★☆☆
Wild adults are quite expensive and rarely seen nowadays. Farmed youngsters are very cheap but often poor quality; look for slightly dearer home-bred stock.

▶ *This is the basic BB (Blue-Black) zebra cichlid. There is also a 'red-top' (red dorsal) form. BB males also exhibit other, more minor, geographical variations.*

HOW do I sex it?
The sexes are differently coloured, with local variations and different colour morphs in both sexes. Males are more likely to have eggspots.

WHAT kind of tank?
Mbuna-only community aquarium.

WHAT minimum size tank?
90x30x45cm, but larger preferred.

WHAT kind of water?
Moderately hard, alkaline (pH7.5+), well-oxygenated, and minimal nitrogenous compounds.

HOW warm?
25-27°C.

WHAT decor?
Vast amounts of rockwork providing numerous caves.

WHAT area of the tank?
Males are fairly bottom orientated in their choice of cave; females swim at all levels.

HOW many in one tank?
Only one male (except in very large tanks), but several females if desired.

HOW does it behave?

Relatively peaceful in mbuna terms, and males hardly ever harass females.

WILL it breed in an aquarium?

Yes, easy to breed if correctly maintained. It is a maternal mouthbrooder, and females can be allowed to brood in the community or be removed to a brooding tank (where the fry are easier to catch).

▶ *Females are brown or (as here) OB (Orange Blotch); the shade of orange and amount of blotching vary.*

▶ *The Marmalade Cat (a corruption of the local name) is the rare male equivalent of OB.*

▼ *The 'Red Zebra' is a completely different species, M. estherae, here a female.*

Neolamprologus brichardi

Fairy cichlid

FISH PROFILE

Not colourful, but one of the easiest, most readily available, most elegant and behaviourally most interesting of dwarf Tanganyikan cichlids.

WHAT size?
Males up to 7cm, females up to 5cm.

WHAT does it eat?
In nature, aquatic invertebrates. Best fed on live and frozen foods in the aquarium, but will take flake.

WHERE is it from?
Lake Tanganyika, East Africa.

WHAT does it cost?
★★☆☆☆ ★★★☆☆
Tank-breds are fairly cheap and readily available, wild specimens are more expensive.

HOW do I sex it?
Only with difficulty and practice. Buy half a dozen and let them sort it out.

WHAT kind of tank?
Species tank or Tanganyika cichlid community aquarium.

WHAT minimum size tank?
60x30x45cm for a pair in a species tank.

WHAT kind of water?
Hard, alkaline (pH8+), well-oxygenated, and minimal nitrogenous compounds.

HOW warm?
25-27°C.

WHAT decor?
Copious rockwork with plenty of small caves at substrate level.

WHAT area of the tank?
Bottom to middle levels.

HOW many in one tank?
This species lives colonially in nature and can be kept this way in a large aquarium. Males will sometimes mate with multiple females. Allow at least 45cm of tank length per pair/harem.

HOW does it behave?
Rather peaceful, though will see off much larger fish in defence of its fry.

WILL it breed in an aquarium?
Yes, though it can be slow to get started. Don't remove the young until they measure about 2.5cm, as they help guard the next brood(s) and the adults may stop spawning for a long time if deprived of their family.

▼ N. brichardi *is also known as the 'Princess of Burundi', or more prosaically, the 'Bric'.*

Nimbochromis livingstonii

Kaligono ('the sleeper')

FISH PROFILE

The Malawi common name reflects the hunting behaviour of this popular aquarium fish in its natural habitat. It lies on its side on the bottom, where the blotches camouflage its outline while the light areas catch the eye of the inquisitive young fishes on which it preys. When a victim draws near, the sleeper awakes and grabs it.

▲ Nimbochromis *means 'cloud cichlid', referring to the irregular blotched, cloudlike pattern.*

WHAT size?
To about 22cm, usually smaller.

WHAT does it eat?
Naturally a piscivore (eats fry), so raw fish should be the main diet, along with shrimp, prawn and earthworms. Avoid too much dry food, which may cause 'bloat'.

WHERE is it from?
Endemic to Lake Malawi, East Africa.

WHAT does it cost?
★☆☆☆☆   ★★★☆☆
Tank-bred youngsters are fairly cheap, wild adults more expensive.

HOW do I sex it?
Males are usually a little larger and change colour to predominantly dark blue during the breeding season.

WHAT kind of tank?
Malawi community with other largish sand-dwellers or open-water species.

WHAT minimum size tank?
120x45x45cm.

WHAT kind of water?
Moderately hard, alkaline (pH 7.5+), well-oxygenated, and minimal nitrogenous compounds.

HOW warm?
25-27°C.

WHAT decor?
Open sand or gravel with occasional rocks, and *Vallisneria* if desired.

WHAT area of the tank?
Strictly a bottom-dweller.

HOW many in one tank?
No limits within normal stocking rules.

HOW does it behave?
Very peaceful for its size, even when breeding.

WILL it breed in an aquarium?
An easy-to-breed maternal mouthbrooder.

Pelvicachromis pulcher

Krib

FISH PROFILE

The nearest thing to the ideal beginner's cichlid – small, colourful, fairly peaceful; easy to keep, sex, and breed; and the brood care is excellent entertainment for all the family.

WHAT size?
Males up to 8cm, females up to 6.5cm.

WHAT does it eat?
In nature, aquatic invertebrates; in captivity, any suitably sized omnivore foods.

WHERE is it from?
The coastal lowlands of Nigeria.

WHAT does it cost?
★☆☆☆☆   ★★☆☆☆
Tank-breds are cheap and often free from breeders, but wild adults are more expensive.

DIFFERENT FORMS
P. pulcher contains several distinct forms, each with minor geographical variations. The aquarium 'krib' and the 'Red' form are just two of these. The former is descended from imports of a single population in the 1960s.

▶ *A pair of kribs; male at bottom.*

HOW do I sex it?
Males are larger and have spots in the tail and pointed pelvic fins. Females are much deeper bodied, have no caudal spots, and club-shaped pelvic fins.

WHAT kind of tank?
Species tank or general community aquarium.

WHAT minimum size tank?
60x30x30cm for a pair alone, 90x30x30cm community aquarium.

WHAT kind of water?
Ideally, soft and slightly acid (pH6.5-6.8), but will do well and breed in hard water too.

▶ *A male* Pelvicachromis *'Red', which may be a separate species.*

HOW warm?
23.5-27°C.

WHAT decor?
A well-planted tank with flowerpot caves.

WHAT area of the tank?
Strictly a bottom-dweller.

HOW many in one tank?
One pair (plus family), except in very large tanks.

HOW does it behave?
Peaceful, but will vigorously defend its brood against any fish that comes near.

WILL it breed in an aquarium?
Yes, very easy to breed. Note that pH6.5-6.8 produces males and females in near-equal numbers; lower or higher pH, more females or males respectively. Brood care continues for months.

▼ *Female P.* pulcher *'Red' usually have a caudal ocellus, unlike in standard kribs. The club-shaped pelvic fins confirm that it is a female fish.*

45

Steatocranus casuarius

Blockhead, lumphead

Although it will never win a beauty contest, this peaceful and easy-to-keep species is an ideal first cichlid for the beginner, but with plenty of interest for the specialist as well.

WHAT size?
Males up to 13cm, females a little smaller.

WHAT does it eat?
Algae and aquatic invertebrates in nature, but accepts all normal aquarium foods.

WHERE is it from?
Lower Congo rapids, West Africa.

WHAT does it cost?
★☆☆☆☆   ★★☆☆☆
Usually cheap, as mainly tank-bred by hobbyists.

HOW do I sex it?
Males are larger and have longer fins and larger humps, but as these differences are relative, sexing isn't easy.

WHAT kind of tank?
Species tank; rapids cichlids community; or general community of medium-sized, peaceful fishes.

WHAT minimum size tank?
60x30x30cm for a pair in a species tank.

WHAT kind of water?
Ideally soft and slightly acid (pH6-6.8), but will thrive and breed in hard water too. High oxygen levels are important.

HOW warm?
23.5-25.5°C.

WHAT decor?
Ideally, water-worn boulders, but unfussy as long as some sort of cave is available.

WHAT area of the tank?
Exclusively a bottom-dweller, but may 'perch' on rocks.

HOW many in one tank?
Allow at least 45cm of tank length per pair.

HOW does it behave?
Because its swimbladder is atrophied, this fish 'hops' around instead of swimming – this is perfectly normal. Very peaceful, even when breeding.

WILL it breed in an aquarium?
Yes, easy to breed if given a cave of some description. As normally only juveniles are available, it is best to start with five or six and let them pair naturally.

▲ *No beauty, but a very peaceful, easy and interesting cichlid.*

Teleogramma brichardi

▶ *A female T. brichardi in breeding coloration.*

A very unusual cichlid in both appearance and behaviour, specially adapted to life in rapids. Although it looks uninteresting in normal coloration, breeding females are stunning.

WHAT size?
Males to around 8cm, females usually slightly smaller.

WHAT does it eat?
The diet in nature is aquatic invertebrates, and in captivity the fish prefers live or frozen live foods. Loves small earthworms.

WHERE is it from?
Lower Congo rapids, West Africa.

WHAT does it cost?
★★☆☆☆　★★★☆☆
Only wild fish are normally available.

HOW do I sex it?
Females have a broad white area in the upper lobe of the tail, males only a narrow white edging.

WHAT kind of tank?
Species tank or rapids cichlids community.

WHAT minimum size tank?
90x30x30cm for a pair in a species tank. Depth is unimportant as these fishes rarely stray far from the bottom.

WHAT kind of water?
Ideally very soft and slightly acid. High oxygen levels are important.

HOW warm?
23.5-25.5°C.

WHAT decor?
Rocks (ideally, large water-worn boulders) arranged to form substrate-level caves. The substrate should be fine sand, as these cichlids burrow head-first under rocks.

WHAT area of the tank?
Exclusively a bottom-dweller, but sometimes likes to survey its territory from the top of a rock.

HOW many in one tank?
Can be kept as a pair or a male with a harem. No more than one male, except in very large tanks.

HOW does it behave?
Because its swimbladder is atrophied, this fish 'hops' instead of swimming. Can be very quarrelsome when settling in and establishing territory, and a divider may be required initially. Can jump out of tanks and over dividers that don't reach the cover glass!

WILL it breed in an aquarium?
Yes, but only a handful of people have achieved this. The main problem is avoiding one of the pair (usually the female) being killed during the establishing of territories. It is a cave-brooding substrate-spawner. The eggs are enormous, cream-coloured and few in number.

Tilapia buttikoferi

Buttie

▶ *Always on the lookout for food!*

FISH PROFILE

A large, beautiful-looking fish, formerly in great demand but less popular now that the downside of the species, particularly male behaviour, is better known. Makes a good pet if kept singly.

WHAT size?
Males up to about 25cm, females smaller.

WHAT does it eat?
Like most tilapias, anything and everything.

WHERE is it from?
Coastal West Africa, from Liberia to Guinea Bissau.

WHAT does it cost?
★☆☆☆☆   ★★★☆☆
Cheap (or even free to good homes), though large show specimens may command a higher price.

HOW do I sex it?
Males are larger and far more aggressive than females. The female is the corpse in any pair.

WHAT kind of tank?
Males in species tanks only, females will get along fine with other largish fish, including other cichlids.

WHAT minimum size tank?
90x45x45cm for a single male, 120x45x45cm upwards for a pair, or for female(s) with other species.

WHAT kind of water?
Apparently indestructible in any type of water.

HOW warm?
24-27°C.

WHAT decor?
Not critical, but note that plants are likely to be vandalised.

WHAT area of the tank?
All, with a preference for the feeding place!

HOW many in one tank?
No more than one male, or a pair. Multiple females are usually OK together.

HOW does it behave?
Most males are utter thugs where other fish are concerned, females are relatively harmless.

WILL it breed in an aquarium?
Yes, but because of the male's aggressive behaviour a divider of some type is normally required to protect the female. Broods are huge, and difficult to sell.

▲ *A male 'buttie', beautiful but bad!*

Tropheus duboisi

Duboisi

FISH PROFILE

This species has arguably the most attractive young of any cichlid, and no more than a dozen of them at a time. Adults are less stunning, but nonetheless highly desirable fishes. Three forms are known, with white, narrow yellow, and broad yellow bands, and young with spots to match.

WHAT size?
Males exceptionally to 12.5cm, females about 8cm.

WHAT does it eat?
In nature, algae and any invertebrates it contains. Feed an omnivore diet with plenty of 'greens'. Too much dried food may result in the fatal disease 'Malawi bloat'.

WHERE is it from?
Rocky shoreline in the northern part of Lake Tanganyika.

WHAT does it cost?
★★★☆☆ ★★★★☆
Both adults and young are expensive, as demand far outstrips supply.

The polka-dot pattern makes young duboisi bestsellers.

HOW do I sex it?
Usually with difficulty, although males lose their spots first and may also lose the band completely.

WHAT kind of tank?
Species tank (best in groups), or sharing with other medium-sized, relatively peaceful Tanganyikan cichlids. Can also be kept with some Malawi cichlids.

WHAT minimum size tank?
120x45x45cm.

WHAT kind of water?
Hard, alkaline (pH8+), well-oxygenated, and minimal nitrogenous compounds.

Adults (here a male) are less attractive, but still greatly in demand.

HOW warm?
24-27°C.

WHAT decor?
Masses of rocks.

WHAT area of the tank?
Anywhere there are rocks.

HOW many in one tank?
No limit within normal stocking rules – the main limitation is cost.

HOW does it behave?
Adults are usually peaceful, but males may fight, and occasionally males harass females. Far less troublesome than some other *Tropheus* spp.

WILL it breed in an aquarium?
Breeding this maternal mouthbrooder is a rare privilege and may involve a long wait for success, as early clutches are often infertile. But the wait is well worthwhile.

49

Xenotilapia flavipinnis

Xenotilapia are among the less commonly seen cichlids from Lake Tanganyika. There are both rock- and sand-dwelling species – the one featured here belongs to the latter group.

▶ *In* X. flavipinnis *the sexes are identical in appearance.*

WHAT size?
Males and females to around 9cm.

WHAT does it eat?
In nature, aquatic invertebrates sifted from the sand. Live and frozen foods are usually necessary in the aquarium, although these fishes may learn to take prepared foods.

WHERE is it from?
Lake Tanganyika, East Africa, in sandy habitats around the lake.

WHAT does it cost?
★★★☆☆ ★★★★☆
Wild fish are expensive, and tank-breds rarely seen.

HOW do I sex it?
Virtually impossible to sex except by the instinct born of experience.

WHAT kind of tank?
Best kept in a group in a very large aquarium so that pairs can form naturally; this species can be mixed with other sand-dwellers.

WHAT minimum size tank?
90x45x45cm for a pair, 180x45x45cm upwards for a group or sharing with other species.

WHAT kind of water?
Hard, alkaline (pH 8+), well-oxygenated, minimal nitrogenous compounds, no strong currents.

HOW warm?
25-27°C.

WHAT decor?
Fine, siftable sand with the occasional rock, NOT mountains of rockwork. A rocky background can be used for (human) aesthetic reasons.

WHAT area of the tank?
Mainly near the bottom.

HOW many in one tank?
One pair unless the tank is huge.

HOW does it behave?
Quite territorial when breeding, but not excessively aggressive. A group will shoal together when not breeding.

WILL it breed in an aquarium?
A biparental mouthbrooder in which the female broods for the first 7-12 days and then the male completes the brooding of the larvae. Not often bred, probably because it is not widely kept. This may be a reflection of its price and requirement for a large, sparsely decorated tank.

Etroplus maculatus

Orange chromide

FISH PROFILE

One of only a very few cichlids found in Asia, this fish can be kept in fresh or brackish water. In nature it lives in a fascinating symbiosis with its larger relative *E. suratensis*, the green chromide.

WHAT size?
Males and females to 9.5cm.

WHAT does it eat?
Carnivorous – the natural diet includes fish eggs and fry. Will take all suitable aquarium foods.

WHERE is it from?
Coastal areas in southern India and Sri Lanka.

WHAT does it cost?
★☆☆☆☆   ★★☆☆☆
Inexpensive.

HOW do I sex it?
Males are larger, females have white markings on the upper and lower edges of the tail, especially when breeding.

WHAT kind of tank?
Species tank or general community of similar-sized fishes.

WHAT minimum size tank?
60x30x30cm species tank, 120x40x40cm general community, with one pair in each case.

WHAT kind of water?
Moderately hard to very hard, pH7.5 or higher. The addition of common salt is beneficial.

HOW warm?
25.5-28°C.

WHAT decor?
Rock and/or flowerpot caves, weathered bogwood. Grass-like plants (e.g. *Vallisneria*) in fresh water, plastic plants in brackish.

WHAT area of the tank?
Bottom.

HOW many in one tank?
Normally one pair, but pairs live close together in nature so a group can be kept in a large species tank.

HOW does it behave?
Relatively peaceful but able to look after itself. Will prodate on fry of other species or other pairs of chromides.

WILL it breed in an aquarium?
Easy to breed. Spawns on sea-grass leaves or stones in the wild. Brood care lasts for many months, apparently a defence against intraspecific predation in nature.

▶ *The coloration of this species ranges from yellow (as shown here) to deep orange.*

Something for everyone

▶ Probably the most popular catfishes in the hobby today belong to the Corydoradinae group, known as corys. The group encompasses 170 species, with new discoveries appearing almost daily. Corys are very peaceful fishes. Some have striking colour patterns, others intriguing habits and in the main, they are reasonably easy to breed. Ranging in size from 2cm to 10cm, they are well suited to aquarium life.

Catfishes in the Loricariidae group vary in size, colour and form. There are many undescribed species, some of which are very colourful. The popularity of Loricariids is due principally to the fabulous colour patterns seen in many species. If you are looking for a more bizarre species, consider the tiny anchor catfish *(Hara jerdoni)* or the banjo catfish *(Dysichthys coracoideus)*. There are more than enough species available to maintain a lifelong interest in catfishes as a whole.

Price guide

★	Up to £5
★★	£5 – £25
★★★	£25 – £50
★★★★	£50 – £100
★★★★★	£100 +

FISH PROFILE

Small specimens are very attractive. The sooty-black body and fins are adorned with brilliant white spots and blotches, making this fish very desirable amongst hobbyists. However, as it grows the white markings become smaller and less prominent. The whole body is covered by a series of thorny, bony plates.

WHAT size?
Males 100cm, females a little smaller.

WHAT does it eat?
Omnivorous. In nature, grazes on the biofilm that covers rocks, roots and fallen branches, searching out insect larvae, zooplankton and shrimps. It is also known as a wood-eater, so provide soft bogwood. Will accept all manner of foods, such as tablets, a variety of vegetables and frozen foods.

WHERE is it from?
The Amazon Basin in Brazil and Peru.

WHAT does it cost?
★★★★☆
This striking fish commands a high price. The star rating is for a 15cm specimen. A 5cm juvenile is less expensive (★★★).

Acanthicus adonis

A juvenile with bold spotting and well-developed protective thorny body scutes. The spots fade with age.

HOW warm?
22-27°C.

WHAT decor?
A gravel substrate with rocks and large pieces of bogwood.

WHAT area of the tank?
Constantly patrols all areas of the aquarium.

HOW many in one tank?
One only.

HOW does it behave?
Regarded as peaceful, but in truth it likes to be the boss and will stamp its authority when its position is challenged. Large cichlids and characins would make ideal tankmates.

WILL it breed in an aquarium?
No known records of captive breeding.

HOW do I sex it?
Males tend to grow larger than females, but that factor alone would be difficult to assess. The odontodes (bristles) that adorn the pectoral fin spines are more prominent in mature males.

WHAT kind of tank?
A very large community or a single-specimen, species-only aquarium.

WHAT minimum size tank?
200x100x100cm.

WHAT kind of water?
Clean, good-quality, soft and slightly acidic (pH6-7), with good movement.

The head and body are laterally compressed. The large pectoral fins have strong spines with sharp bristles.

Amblydoras hancockii

Talking, or croaking, catfish

FISH PROFILE

This species gets its common name from the sound it makes by agitating the pectoral fin spine in its socket, which resonates through the swimbladder. Handle the fish with caution, as the pectoral fin spines are very strong and heavily serrated. They are used as a defensive mechanism to lock the fish into crevices or to grip objects. They will cause serious damage if clamped onto a misplaced finger.

WHAT size?
Males and females 12.5cm.

WHAT does it eat?
In the wild its diet includes worm and insect larvae. Readily accepts tablet, granular and frozen foods.

WHERE is it from?
Algae-rich waters in Brazil, Colombia and Guyana.

WHAT does it cost?
★★☆☆☆
Moderately priced.

▼ *When disturbed, the thick pectoral spines are rotated in their sockets, creating a croaking sound.*

HOW do I sex it?
Females are a dirty white on the underside, wheras males are speckled.

WHAT kind of tank?
A well-lit, shallow, specialist aquarium is best, but would be happy in the clear water of any community aquarium.

WHAT minimum size tank?
80x25x20cm.

WHAT kind of water?
Good-quality, slightly to medium hard, slightly acidic to slightly alkaline (pH6-7.5). Heavy with algae is desirable but not essential.

HOW warm?
22-26°C.

WHAT decor?
A sandy substrate, a few pieces of bogwood to create shady places and some broadleaved plants.

WHAT area of the tank?
Bottom-dweller.

HOW many in one tank?
Two, preferably a pair.

HOW does it behave?
Very peaceful, suitable for any community aquarium.

WILL it breed in an aquarium?
There are no reports of this species being bred in captivity, but observations in the wild show that the fish build a bubblenest amongst the surface plants and that the male takes sole parental responsibility.

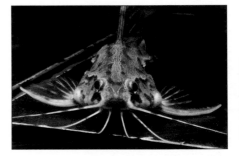

▲ *The talking catfish uses its long, sensitive barbels to detect food in the sandy substrate.*

Ancistrus temminckii

Bristlenose catfish

FISH PROFILE

It is difficult to determine the true identity of the so-called *Ancistrus temminckii* available today, without being able to compare specimens from the type locality in Surinam with those already in the hobby. It is quite possible that the specimens on sale are, in fact, hybrids created within the hobby. A number of very similar-looking species inhabit most of the Amazon region. To add more confusion, there is also an albino form, which may or may not be the same species. Whatever their true identity, they are intriguing, relatively easy to breed and well worth keeping.

WHAT size?
Males and females 10cm.

WHAT does it eat?
In nature, algae, zooplankton, insect larvae and small crustaceans. Readily accepts tablet, wafer and frozen foods.

WHERE is it from?
The type specimen was described from Surinam, but it is reportedly widespread throughout northern Brazil.

WHAT does it cost?
★☆☆☆☆
Inexpensive.

HOW do I sex it?
Mature males have longer, branched, soft bristles that grow down the centre and around the sides of the head. The female bristles are short and unbranched.

WHAT kind of tank?
Community or specimen aquarium.

WHAT minimum size tank?
60x30x30cm.

WHAT kind of water?
Good-quality, but tolerates a wide range of conditions, from soft/acid to hard/mildly alkaline (pH5.8-8).

HOW warm?
21-24°C.

WHAT decor?
A sandy or fine gravel substrate, with rocks, pieces of tree root or bogwood to create caves and shady hiding places. If soft bogwood is included in the decor, provide a good filtering system or carry out regular siphoning to remove the copious amounts of wood mulm produced by the fish through their perpetual grazing.

WHAT area of the tank?
All, but mainly occupies the bottom areas under or amongst pieces of wood. Will also graze on the algae that forms on the aquarium glass.

HOW many in one tank?
One pair.

HOW does it behave?
Very peaceful, but may damage plants.

WILL it breed in an aquarium?
Yes, regularly. Males like to occupy caves or tight-fitting spaces, where they encourage a female to join them. Once the female has laid her bright-orange eggs, which can number over 100, the male takes full responsibility for looking after them. They hatch in 11-12 days.

▼ *A male showing a very good set of bristles. It is said that these are seen by the female as a sign of a good parent and she will usually pick the male with the best set of bristles to mate with.*

Brochis splendens

Emerald catfish

FISH PROFILE

This is a beautiful fish, aptly named emerald catfish, because of its all-over, brilliant metallic-green body colour. Being primarily a bottom-dweller, it is ideally suited for that position in any community aquarium.

WHAT size?
At 7.6cm, *B. splendens* is the smallest of the three *Brochis* species. Unlike many other members of the family Corydoradinae, there is very little difference in size between the sexes.

WHAT does it eat?
Readily accepts flake, tablet, granular and frozen foods. Tubifex, bloodworm, whiteworm and daphnia will help to keep it in tiptop condition.

WHERE is it from?
Fairly widespread from central Brazil west to Peru and Ecuador.

WHAT does it cost?
★★☆☆
Moderately priced.

▶ *Good barbels are a sign that the fish is healthy and that conditions are right.*

HOW do I sex it?
Males have longer, more pointed pelvic fins. Females are broader in the body.

WHAT kind of tank?
Mixed community or specialist breeding tank.

WHAT minimum size tank?
60x30x30cm.

WHAT kind of water?
Tolerates a wide range of water conditions, pH5.6-7.6.

HOW warm?
22-27°C.

WHAT decor?
Smooth-grained sand substrate, with pieces of bogwood and/or smooth rocks. Well-§planted, with some large-leaved, overhanging plants to create shade and potential egglaying sites.

▲ *A fine male emerald catfish. Juveniles display a greatly exaggerated dorsal fin and are often imported as 'sailfin corys'.*

WHAT area of the tank?
Mainly bottom, with forays to the water surface and amongst the plant leaves.

HOW many in one tank?
Group of six.

HOW does it behave?
Very peaceful and moderately active. Spends most of its time with its nose buried in the sandy substrate, searching for food.

WILL it breed in an aquarium?
A challenge, but it can be achieved. Pairs come together in the classic 'T' mating clinch and, after a spell of group courtship, eggs are usually deposited on the undersides of floating or overhanging leaves.

Corydoras adolfoi
Adolfoi's cory

FISH PROFILE

A beautiful species, with a tan-coloured body, sooty-black eye mask and broad stripe along the ridge of the back. Its most striking feature is the large, bright-orange patch on the head in front of the dorsal fin. A group makes an impressive sight in any aquarium.

WHAT size?
Males 5.5cm, females 6cm.

WHAT does it eat?
In nature, insect larvae, shrimps, worms and crustaceans. In the aquarium, readily accepts flake, tablet, granular and frozen foods. Live daphnia, bloodworm or tubifex help to bring it into breeding condition.

WHERE is it from?
Brazil, tributaries of the upper Rio Negro, Nouba Ouba creek, Sao Gabriel da Cachoeira.

WHAT does it cost?
★★☆☆☆
Moderately priced.

HOW do I sex it?
Males are a little smaller and have longer, more pointed pelvic fins; females are broader and deeper in the body.

WHAT kind of tank?
Community or specialist aquarium.

WHAT minimum size tank?
60x30x30cm.

WHAT kind of water?
Good-quality, well-filtered, soft and acidic water would be preferable, especially if breeding is to be attempted, but this species will accept a wide range of conditions.

HOW warm?
Prefers slightly higher temperatures, 24-28°C.

WHAT decor?
A fine, smooth-grained, sandy substrate, well-planted, with a few pieces of bogwood to create hiding places and some floating plants to subdue the lighting. Tannins released from the bogwood will give the aquarium a natural blackwater look.

WHAT area of the tank?
Bottom-dwelling; will also forage in all areas of the aquarium and make occasional trips to the surface for a gulp of air.

HOW many in one tank?
Six. A ratio of two males to one females is best, especially if you want to attempt breeding.

HOW does it behave?
Very peaceful, ideal for any community aquarium.

WILL it breed in an aquarium?
Not as easy to breed as many other corys. Pairs come together in the classic 'T' mating clinch, and after a short period of group courtship, females lay up to 60 sticky, 1.8mm-diameter eggs. These are usually deposited amongst the plants and on the aquarium sides.

▲ *A female in top breeding condition. C. adolfoi was one of the first so-called orange-spot species to enter the aquarium hobby.*

Corydoras aeneus

Bronze cory

Originally described from the island of Trinidad, this highly popular cory is very rarely imported from the wild, but is commercially bred by fish farmers in the Far East and exported all over the world. There are albino and long-finned forms, both of which were produced in the aquarium; the latter is man-made and not a natural form. *C. aeneus* is hardy and inexpensive, making it an ideal candidate for the first-time corydoras breeder.

WHAT size?
One of the larger members of the family; males 6.5cm, females 7.5cm.

WHAT does it eat?
In nature, insect larvae, shrimps, worms and crustaceans. In the aquarium, readily accepts flake, tablet, granular and frozen foods. Live daphnia, bloodworm or tubifex help to bring this species into breeding condition.

WHERE is it from?
First described from the clear streams of western Trinidad. So-called variations are found throughout most of South America.

WHAT does it cost?
★☆☆☆☆
One of the cheapest and most readily available *Corydoras*.

HOW do I sex it?
Males have longer, more pointed pelvic fins; females are broader in the body and grow longer.

WHAT kind of tank?
Community aquarium.

WHAT minimum size tank?
60x30x30cm.

WHAT kind of water?
Very tolerant of a wide range of water conditions, from soft/acidic to moderately hard/alkaline, but they should be good quality.

HOW warm?
18-26°C.

WHAT decor?
A fine, smooth-grained sand substrate, well-planted, with pieces of bogwood, smooth stones and some floating plants to create subdued lighting.

▼ *The albino form is one of the most commonly bred* Corydoras *species.*

WHAT area of the tank?
Predominantly a bottom-dweller, often foraging amongst the plants, with an occasional dart to the surface for a gulp of air.

HOW many in one tank?
Six. For breeding, a ratio of two males to one female is best.

HOW does it behave?
Very peaceful, ideal for any community aquarium.

WILL it breed in an aquarium?
Yes, one of the easiest *Corydoras* species to breed. Pairs come together in the classic 'T' mating clinch, and after a spell of group courtship, females deposit their sticky, 1.7mm-diameter eggs on plants, rocks, but mostly on the aquarium sides.

▲ When in good condition, C. aeneus *shows a beautiful golden-bronze body colour.*

NEW SPECIES FROM THE WILD

A number of wild specimens are being imported from various parts of South America, from Argentina in the south to Venezuela in the north. All are called *Corydoras aeneus*, but because of the vastness – and in some cases the isolation – of their range, it is likely that many will eventually prove to be species in their own right.

▼ *At present, this species is considered to be a naturally black colour variant of C. aeneus. However, there are subtle differences in its morphology and breeding habits and it may prove to be a separate species.*

◀ *Although most imports are bred in fish farms, natural albinos are sometimes found.*

Corydoras pygmaeus

Pygmy or dwarf cory

This tiny species, just 2-3cm long, is ideally suited to a small aquarium. In common with many other Corydoradinae species, pygmy corys are by nature shoaling fishes, but their added attraction is a tendency to swim in groups in midwater, especially if there are other groups of small fishes to shoal with.

WHAT size?
Males 2cm, females 3.2cm.

WHAT does it eat?
In nature, feeds on small insect larvae, shrimps and crustaceans. Readily accepts crushed flake, tablet and small frozen foods.

WHERE is it from?
Brazil: Rio Madeira near mouth of Rio Jipirana. Ecuador: Rio Aguarico. Peru: Rio Nanay near Iquitos.

WHAT does it cost?
★☆☆☆☆
Inexpensive.

C NUMBER SYSTEM
Because of the difficulty in recognising many of the new cory discoveries, as well as some existing undescribed species, a coding system – C numbers – has become internationally accepted.

HOW do I sex it?
Females are larger and plumper.

WHAT kind of tank?
Small community or species aquarium.

WHAT minimum size tank?
45x25x25cm.

WHAT kind of water?
Very tolerant of a wide range of conditions, but the water should be clean and well-filtered.

HOW warm?
20-25°C.

WHAT decor?
A fine sandy substrate, well planted with fine-leaved plants. A few large pebbles and/or tree roots.

WHAT area of the tank?
Patrols all areas of the tank.

▲ *Although it is one of the smallest* Corydoras *species,* C. pygmaeus *is full of character.*

HOW many in one tank?
Twelve. Best kept in ratios of two males to one female.

HOW does it behave?
An extremely peaceful little fish.

WILL it breed in an aquarium?
Yes, this is one of the easiest *Corydoras* species to breed once the fish are in tiptop condition. It usually only takes a water change, using slightly cooler water, to trigger spawning activity. A single female will lay up to 20 small, sticky, almost clear eggs, which she deposits all over the aquarium, on the glass or amongst the plant leaves. The fry take four days to hatch and are usually ignored by the adult fish.

Corydoras sterbai

Sterba's cory

FISH PROFILE

Corydoras sterbai has been regularly available in the hobby for a number of years. It is fairly easy to breed, yet still commands a respectable asking price in aquarium shops. It also one of the most beautiful *Corydoras* species, with its silvery white body covered with darker grey-brown spots, blotches and wavy lines, highlighted by the bright yellow/orange pectoral and pelvic fin spines. As it prefers warmer conditions, it makes an ideal tankmate for discus.

WHAT size?
Moderately large species, males 6cm, females 6.5cm.

WHAT does it eat?
In nature, feeds on insect larvae, shrimps, worms and crustaceans. Readily accepts flake, tablet, granular and frozen foods. Live daphnia, bloodworm or tubifex help to bring it into breeding condition.

WHERE is it from?
Brazil, State of Mato Grosso, upper Rio Guapore.

WHAT does it cost?
★★☆☆☆
Moderately priced.

HOW do I sex it?
Males are a little smaller and have longer, more pointed pelvic fins; females are broader and deeper in the body.

WHAT kind of tank?
Ideal for community aquariums with warmth-loving species.

WHAT minimum size tank?
60x30x30cm.

WHAT kind of water?
Good-quality and well-filtered. Will accept a wide range of conditions but a pH range of 5.6 to 7.4 would be best.

HOW warm?
Much prefers higher temperatures, 25-30ºC.

WHAT decor?
A fine, smooth-grained, sandy substrate, well planted. Include a few pieces of bogwood or tree roots to create plenty of hiding places and some floating plants to subdue the lighting.

WHAT area of the tank?
Predominantly bottom-dwelling, but forages in all areas and makes occasional trips to the surface for a gulp of air.

HOW many in one tank?
Group of six. A ratio of two males to one female is best, especially for breeding.

HOW does it behave?
Very peaceful, ideal for any community aquarium.

WILL it breed in an aquarium?
Yes, reasonably easy to breed. Pairs come together in the classic 'T' mating clinch, and after a spell of group courtship, females lay up to 250 sticky, 1.7mm-diameter eggs. These are deposited in every conceivable place around the aquarium, but mostly on the sides and within 5cm of the surface.

▼ *The distinctive bright yellow pectoral and pelvic fin spines make this a very popular* Corydoras *species.*

Corydoras trilineatus

Three-lined cory

FISH PROFILE

This is a fairly common species, imported by the thousand from Peru, and like most *Corydoras* species, very active and full of character. The fish is silvery white, with a striking colour pattern of dark, almost black, wavy lines and blotches on the head and a three-lined pattern along the side of the body. It is a very attractive fish, suitable for any community aquarium.

WHAT size?
A relatively small species, males 5cm, females 6cm.

WHAT does it eat?
Readily accepts flake, tablet, granular and frozen foods. Live daphnia, bloodworm or tubifex help to bring it into breeding condition.

WHERE is it from?
Peru, the tributaries of the Rio Ambyiacu.

WHAT does it cost?
★☆☆☆☆
An inexpensive species.

HOW do I sex it?
Males have longer, more pointed pelvic fins; females are broader in the body and grow longer.

WHAT kind of tank?
Community aquarium or specialist breeding tank.

WHAT minimum size tank?
45x25x25cm.

WHAT kind of water?
Good-quality, medium-soft, neutral to slightly acid (pH6.5-7).

HOW warm?
22-28°C.

WHAT decor?
Sandy substrate, with pieces of bogwood or smooth stones.

WHAT area of the tank?
Bottom, with occasional forays to the surface for a gulp of air, or into the plant leaves in a constant search for food.

HOW many in one tank?
Group of six, with a ratio of two males to every female.

HOW does it behave?
Very peaceful, an ideal species for any community aquarium.

WILL it breed in an aquarium?
Yes, relatively easily. After a spell of group courtship, pairs come together in the classic 'T' mating clinch. Eggs may be deposited on plant leaves, rocks, but mostly on the sides or, more specifically, in the corners of the aquarium.

▼ *The distinctive colour pattern of C. trilineatus is clearly shown in this example. However, a considerable amount of colour variation is found even in a single population, which can cause problems with identification.*

▲ *The pattern can range from bold wavy lines and streaks to quite fine spotting.*

Dianema urostriata
Flagtail catfish

FISH PROFILE

This member of the very popular Callichthyidae, or 'armoured' catfishes, has two rows of bony protective plates, called scutes, running along each side of the body. Its striking whitish tail has up to seven, broad, black, horizontal stripes. This species comes from the acidic 'blackwaters' of the Rio Negro in Brazil, which are low in dissolved ions and contain acidic residues leaching into the water through layers of plant material on the forest floor.

▼ *Bold tail stripes are an attractive feature.*

WHAT size?
Males 11cm, females 12cm.

WHAT does it eat?
The natural diet consists of insect larvae, small crustaceans and worms. Readily accepts flake, tablet and frozen food.

WHERE is it from?
Rio Negro near Manaus in Brazil.

WHAT does it cost?
★★☆☆☆
Moderately priced.

HOW do I sex it?
Males are generally smaller and slimmer-bodied.

WHAT kind of tank?
Biotype community or specimen aquarium.

WHAT minimum size tank?
90x30x38cm.

WHAT kind of water?
Good-quality, dark, peaty, soft acid to neutral water. To create ideal conditions for *D. urostriata*, pass the aquarium water through a peat filter or allow it to stand in a container partially filled with peat.

HOW warm?
23-28°C.

WHAT decor?
A white sandy substrate, with some rocks, planted areas and pieces of bogwood and dead oak leaves to create the perfect 'blackwater' habitat with numerous hiding places.

WHAT area of the tank?
Likes to cruise around the aquarium in groups.

HOW many in one tank?
Keep this shoaling species in groups of at least four.

HOW does it behave?
Very peaceful and safe with smaller fish.

WILL it breed in an aquarium?
Yes, this species has bred in the aquarium, but there are no known published accounts of captive spawnings.

▼ *Sensitive barbels and large eyes help the fish to find food in its shady, blackwater habitat.*

Dysichthys coracoideus

Banjo catfish

▲ *The head of D. coracoideus, showing the very small eye and craggy appearance of this fish.*

FISH PROFILE

'Banjo' catfish aptly describes this unique species with its broad flat head and long narrow body. An easy species to keep and maintain. It spends most of the daylight hours buried in the sand with just the top of its head protruding, lying in wait for any small, unsuspecting fish or insect to venture within reach. Only becomes really active at night, when it cruises the tank looking for food. Occasionally, the banjo perches in the upper reaches of plant thickets.

WHAT size?
Males and females 12cm.

WHAT does it eat?
Bloodworm, tubifex, small earthworms, flake and tablet foods.

WHERE is it from?
Peru: Amazon, Rio Nanay, Rio Ucayali. Brazil: Amazonas, Rio Jutahay.

WHAT does it cost?
★★☆☆☆
Moderately priced.

▶ *Viewed from above, it is easy to see how the banjo catfish acquired its common name.*

HOW do I sex it?
No visual sexual differences.

WHAT kind of tank?
Community or specialist aquarium.

WHAT minimum size tank?
60x30x25cm.

WHAT kind of water?
Good-quality, well-filtered water is essential, but the parameters are not critical.

HOW warm?
23-26°C.

▼ *During the day, only the tip of the snout, the eyes and the bumps on top of the head are visible.*

WHAT decor?
A fine sandy substrate is essential, with some oak or beech leaf litter. Plants and pieces of bogwood.

WHAT area of the tank?
Bottom-dweller.

HOW many in one tank?
Group of six.

HOW does it behave?
A generally very peaceful, nocturnal species that is almost totally inactive during the day. However, it is a predator that will take small fish, such as young livebearer fry.

WILL it breed in an aquarium?
Over the years there have been many attempts to breed this fish, with some successes being reported, but there are no records to be found, probably because its secretive and nocturnal nature make observations of its behaviour difficult.

Glyptoperichthys gibbiceps
Sailfin pleco

FISH PROFILE

A magnificent fish when fully grown, with its dark, rich-brown colour pattern, and especially when it carries its large sail-like dorsal fin erect. The problems start when the fish is small – 7.5cm – and sold as an ideal 'algae-eater'. This is true, but it is potentially a large fish that needs plenty of room. Be sure to take this into account when making a purchase.

WHAT size?
Males and females up to about 50cm.

WHAT does it eat?
An omnivore; in nature, grazes on algae, insect larvae, shrimps and small crustaceans. In the aquarium it accepts tablet, wafer, granulated and all manner of frozen foods.

WHERE is it from?
Brazil, Amazonas State, Rio Negro.

WHAT does it cost?
★☆☆☆☆
Inexpensive when small.

HOW do I sex it?
No obvious sexual differences, although some Loricariidae experts say sexing can be achieved by examining the genital papillae; in females, it is rounded and in males, elongated.

WHAT kind of tank?
A large community or species-only aquarium.

WHAT minimum size tank?
Community aquarium: 120x45x45cm. Species-only aquarium for a single specimen on its own: 90x45x45cm.

WHAT kind of water?
Good-quality, well-filtered, but the parameters are not critical.

HOW warm?
22-27°C.

WHAT decor?
A gravel substrate and plenty of pieces of bogwood, creating dense areas. If used at all, plants should be robust species, grown in pots to avoid being uprooted.

WHAT area of the tank?
In subdued lighting, this fish will patrol most areas of the aquarium.

HOW many in one tank?
One only.

HOW does it behave?
Despite its large mature size, it is generally peaceful. The only time there may be problems is if another fish occupies a space it wants for itself; then it will usually just muscle its way in.

WILL it breed in an aquarium?
No known breeding accounts.

▲ A 'gibby' showing off its impressive, sail-like dorsal fin.

65

Hara jerdoni
Anchor catfish

FISH PROFILE

This demure little catfish gets its common name from the fact that when locked, its very large pectoral fin spines resemble the anchor of a sailing ship.

WHAT size?
Males 3cm, females 3.3cm.

WHAT does it eat?
Favours live foods in the form of small bloodworms, grindalworm, sifted daphnia, tubifex and brineshrimp. Can be encouraged to eat flake and tablets, but be sure to remove uneaten food.

WHERE is it from?
Oxygen-rich rivers and streams of northern India and Bangladesh.

WHAT does it cost?
★★☆☆☆
Moderately priced.

▶ *With its outstretched pectoral fins, H. jerdoni looks just like the anchor of an old sailing ship.*

HOW do I sex it?
Females grow a little larger and plumper. The male's pectoral fins are usually more pronounced.

WHAT kind of tank?
Ideal for a community tank.

WHAT minimum size tank?
45x25x25cm.

WHAT kind of water?
Top-quality, highly oxygenated, soft, neutral (pH7) water is essential. Good water movement is beneficial but not essential.

HOW warm?
18-23°C.

WHAT decor?
A fine, sandy substrate with pieces of bogwood, tree roots, rocks and a group of fine-leaved plants.

WHAT area of the tank?
Bottom-dweller. Spends much of its time under rocks and amongst roots, but becomes more active as daylight fades, searching for food.

HOW many in one tank?
Two or three pairs.

HOW does it behave?
Very peaceful and timid. Keep with tankmates of a similar size.

WILL it breed in an aquarium?
Yes, a few specialist fishkeepers are now breeding this species under aquarium conditions. Because of its nocturnal and very secretive nature, information is sparse. Females produce about 30 eggs, which they deposit in clumps of Java moss or spawning mops. Young start to emerge after three days.

Hypancistrus zebra

Zebra plec

FISH PROFILE

This strikingly patterned species has now become very expensive in the hobby and scarce in its natural habitat; so much so that the Brazilian government has put a total ban on collecting and exporting it. For those who can afford it, this fish is well worth the effort of setting up a specialist breeding aquarium. Eventually, captive breeding will be the only way this species will remain in the hobby.

The classic display of a male 'zebra' makes it one of the most desirable of all catfishes.

WHAT size?
Males and females approximately 7cm.

WHAT does it eat?
Small pieces of lean beef, chopped mussels, insect larvae and proprietary cichlid foods. Live or frozen bloodworms are a favourite food.

WHERE is it from?
The Rio Xingu in Brazil. Lives at depths of up to 18m amongst the crevices and caves formed in the lava rocks.

WHAT does it cost?
★★★★★
Very expensive, irrespective of size.

HOW do I sex it?
Not always easy. Males tend to be broader in the head, with prominent bristles on the pectoral fins; they may also show reddish tips to their pectoral and pelvic fins when in breeding condition. Females tend to have a more pointed head shape and be a little broader in the body.

WHAT kind of tank?
Although fairly hardy, best kept in a specialist aquarium.

WHAT minimum size tank?
60x30x30cm.

WHAT kind of water?
Very good-quality, turbulent. Preferably soft, slightly acidic.

HOW warm?
27-32ºC.

WHAT decor?
Sandy substrate with rocks and slate arranged in plenty of small snug caves for the male fish. Subdued lighting is more natural.

WHAT area of the tank?
Usually stays hidden amongst the rocks or in caves, venturing out to feed.

HOW many in one tank?
Eight.

HOW does it behave?
Completely peaceful; males may squabble amongst themselves when selecting the best caves.

WILL it breed in an aquarium?
Yes, regularly, but not considered easy. Females are attracted into the male's caves, where they deposit a small number eggs and depart, leaving the male to look after the eggs until they hatch.

Viewed from any angle, Hypancistrus zebra is a beautiful fish.

Leiarus marmoratus

Marbled catfish

FISH PROFILE

Kept as a specimen fish, the marbled catfish will become quite tame and may even accept food offered by hand. Its mature size makes it suitable only for the dedicated aquarist who can provide it with adequate accommodation. It has graceful sleek lines and a beautiful dark and light brown marbled pattern over its entire body and fins. The very long barbels, which can reach back as far as the caudal fin, are always on the move, sensing food, or just locating objects around the aquarium. This fish has a voracious appetite, and a filter system capable of handling the waste is essential.

WHAT size?
A large species; males and females grow to 60cm.

WHAT does it eat?
A large carnivore that feeds on small fish and aquatic animals in the wild. Aquarium specimens will accept pieces of meat, fish, prawns, earthworms and tablet food.

WHERE is it from?
Venezuela and Brazil.

WHAT does it cost?
★★★★☆
Expensive. Small specimens (7.5cm) are occasionally available and are less expensive (★★★).

▼ An impressive specimen showing its beautiful body pattern and sail-like dorsal fin.

HOW do I sex it?
No visual external differences.

WHAT kind of tank?
Large community or species aquarium.

WHAT minimum size tank?
180x60x60cm.

WHAT kind of water?
Good-quality, clean, well-oxygenated water is essential. It should be soft to medium hard; parameters are not critical, but avoid extremes.

▶ Seen from above, the long barbels can be appreciated in all their glory.

HOW warm?
21-25ºC.

WHAT decor?
Smooth gravel substrate, stones, large pieces of bogwood to provide hiding places, well-anchored, robust plants and floating plants to create subdued lighting in the aquarium.

WHAT area of the tank?
Patrols all areas.

HOW many in one tank?
One only.

HOW does it behave?
A predator that should not be kept with fish smaller than itself.

WILL it breed in an aquarium?
No known records of natural captive breeding.

Leiocassis (Pseudomystus) siamensis
Asian bumblebee catfish

FISH PROFILE

This nocturnal species has long been a favourite with hobbyists. It seeks out the darker, shady areas of the aquarium, where it will spend most of the day, becoming far more active when the lights go out. It has extremely sharp fin spines, which can inflict a painful wound if mishandled.

WHAT size?
A medium-sized species, males and females grow to 20cm.

WHAT does it eat?
The natural diet consists of small crustaceans and insect larvae. It will accept most tablet, granular and flake foods. Frozen bloodworm or mosquito larvae make a very good substitute for live foods.

WHERE is it from?
Cambodia, Thailand.

WHAT does it cost?
★★☆☆☆
Moderately priced.

HOW do I sex it?
No reliable visual differences, but it is reasonably safe to assume that mature females are fuller in the body.

WHAT kind of tank?
Larger community or a specialist species aquarium.

WHAT minimum size tank?
90x30x30cm.

WHAT kind of water?
Well-filtered and good-quality. Tolerates a wide range of water parameters.

HOW warm?
20-27°C.

WHAT decor?
A sand or fine gravel substrate, with pieces of bogwood or tree roots arranged to provide caves. Choose robust plants in pots to avoid uprooting.

WHAT area of the tank?
Constantly patrols all areas of the tank.

HOW many in one tank?
Being territorial, it is best kept singly, although two or three specimens can be housed in a large aquarium furnished with plenty of hiding places.

HOW does it behave?
A mainly nocturnal and highly territorial species that should not be kept with species smaller than itself.

WILL it breed in an aquarium?
No known records of breeding in aquarium conditions.

▲ *This is a beautifully marked adult male. Long known in the hobby as Leiocassis siamensis, this fish has been reclassified in the genus Pseudomystus.*

Liosomadoras oncinus

Jaguar catfish

FISH PROFILE

An interesting, easy-to-keep species with a unique colour pattern that resembles the Jaguar cat *(Panthera onca)*, from which it gets its common name. Quite secretive, but in a low-light environment, it can be encouraged to be more active and cruise the open areas of the aquarium. Colour pattern can be very variable, making each specimen distinctive.

▲ This beautifully marked specimen has the classic jaguar pattern.

WHAT size?
A moderately sized species, both sexes reaching 15cm.

WHAT does it eat?
Not a fussy eater; will accept a variety of foods, including tinned cat food, pieces of lean meat or fish. It has a large mouth and will take quite large offerings.

WHERE is it from?
Brazil: Amazonas state, in Rio Xeruini and Rio Negro.

WHAT does it cost?
★★☆☆☆
Small specimens are moderately priced.

HOW do I sex it?
Mature males have thicker, more robust dorsal and pectoral fin spines. They also possess a genital papilla, which is a modification of the anal fin.

WHAT kind of tank?
Species-only or a community aquarium with fishes of a similar or larger size.

WHAT minimum size tank?
90x30x30cm.

WHAT kind of water?
Good-quality, well-filtered, slightly soft, neutral (pH7).

HOW warm?
23-26°C.

WHAT decor?
A sandy or fine gravel substrate, with large pieces of bogwood creating overhangs and shady areas. Subdued lighting.

WHAT area of the tank?
Patrols all areas, but tends to stay in the shade until the lights go off; then it becomes far more active.

HOW many in one tank?
Four.

HOW does it behave?
Generally peaceful, but will predate on smaller fish. Mature males become more aggressive towards each other when asserting their dominance.

WILL it breed in an aquarium?
It should be possible, but no records are known.

Merodontotus tigrinus

Tiger shovelnose catfish

FISH PROFILE

A beautifully patterned fish with distinctive body stripes. It needs a large aquarium with a powerful filter system that can create the highly oxygenated, fast-moving water it is used to in the wild, so is best suited to the specialist aquarist.

WHAT size?
Moderately large catfish, males and females growing to 50cm.

WHAT does it eat?
A predatory species whose natural diet consists mainly of small fish. In the aquarium, offer it fish, fish meat and prawns. It may take a while to encourage newly imported specimens to eat non-live foods.

WHERE is it from?
Brazil, 'Cachoeiras do Teotonio' rapids in the Rio Madeira.

WHAT does it cost?
★★★★★
Very expensive. Even juveniles command a high price.

HOW do I sex it?
No visual external differences.

WHAT kind of tank?
Community of equally large species, or a specimen tank.

WHAT minimum size tank?
150x60x60cm.

WHAT kind of water?
Good-quality, clean, well-oxygenated water is essential, soft to medium, pH7 (neutral).

HOW warm?
22-27°C.

WHAT decor?
Sand or fine gravel substrate, large pieces of bogwood and rocks to form hiding places, with open swimming areas.

▲ *Tiger shovelnose aptly describes this wide mouthed, broad, flat-headed stripey predator.*

WHAT area of the tank?
Likes to lie in ambush amongst rocks and roots, but will also patrol the whole tank.

HOW many in one tank?
One only.

HOW does it behave?
This predator should only be kept with other large species. Small fish are considered as food and will soon disappear.

WILL it breed in an aquarium?
No records of captive breeding are known.

▲ *With its slender lines and camouflage pattern, this fish is built for speed and stealth.*

Microglanis iheringi

South American bumblebee catfish

FISH PROFILE

Although this species is small enough to suit almost any size of aquarium, has a striking colour pattern and is relatively active, it is nocturnal. However, if given a very shady environment and offered its favourite food, bloodworms, it can be encouraged to become more active during the day.

WHAT size?
Relatively small; males and females 8.5cm.

WHAT does it eat?
In the wild, small crustaceans, bloodworms and insect larvae, but readily accepts most tablet, granular and flake foods. Frozen bloodworm or mosquito larvae make a very good substitute for live foods. However, this fish is a glutton that will gorge itself, so take care to control the amount of food you offer it.

WHERE is it from?
Fairly widespread in Colombia and Venezuela.

WHAT does it cost?
★☆☆☆☆
Inexpensive.

HOW do I sex it?
No reliable visual differences, but it would be safe to assume that mature females are fuller in the body.

WHAT kind of tank?
Community or species-only aquarium.

WHAT minimum size tank?
45x25x25cm.

WHAT kind of water?
Well-filtered and in pristine condition, medium/medium hard, neutral (pH7).

HOW warm?
21-25°C.

WHAT decor?
A heavily planted aquarium with a fine, sandy substrate and a few pieces of bogwood.

▼ *The smallest of the 'bumblebees', showing the typical body markings. Although generally considered peaceful, do not keep this species with fishes less than threequarters its own length.*

WHAT area of the tank?
During the hours of darkness, it patrols all areas of the aquarium in search of food.

HOW many in one tank?
Group of four.

HOW does it behave?
Generally peaceful and will not harm its tankmates, but small fishes may be considered as food.

WILL it breed in an aquarium?
No records of captive breeding are known.

SIMILAR 'BUMBLEBEES'

Bumblebee catfish are fairly widespread throughout South America and comprised of two genera, *Microglanis* and *Pseudopimelodus*. They are also similar in colour pattern to the Asian bumblebee catfish (*Pseudomystus siamensis* – see page 69).

Mystus vittatus

Asian striped catfish

FISH PROFILE

An active species that patrols the tank during the day. A large planted aquarium with a shoal of seven or eight specimens is an impressive sight. The fish has four distinctive, thick, dark, candy stripes running the full length of the body, giving it a very sleek appearance. It is a 'naked catfish', which means there are no scales or scutes to protect the body. The skin is quite tough but easily scratched or damaged by sharp objects. Use tank decorations and furnishings with smooth edges.

WHAT size?
Moderately sized, both males and females reach 20cm.

WHAT does it eat?
Not a fussy eater; accepts tablets, flake, fish meat and frozen foods.

WHERE is it from?
India and Pakistan.

WHAT does it cost?
★☆☆☆☆ ★★☆☆☆
Small (7.5cm) specimens are usually inexpensive.

▲ *A good example of* M. vittatus *with well-defined stripes. This is a shoaling species and the fish do best in groups.*

HOW do I sex it?
No visual external differences.

WHAT kind of tank?
Community aquarium.

WHAT minimum size tank?
90x30x30cm.

WHAT kind of water?
Soft to medium hard, slightly acid to neutral (pH6-7).

HOW warm?
22-28°C.

WHAT decor?
A well-planted aquarium with a sandy substrate, pieces of bogwood or tree root to create hiding places and open spaces to provide clear swimming areas.

WHAT area of the tank?
Patrols all areas of the tank.

HOW many in one tank?
Two. Larger groups would be compatible, but house them in larger aquariums.

HOW does it behave?
Generally peaceful, but tankmates should be at least half its size.

WILL it breed in an aquarium?
Yes, reported to lay quite large eggs among tree roots.

73

Pareutropius debauwi

African glass catfish

FISH PROFILE

This is a beautiful, elegant-looking species, with a silvery grey-and-white body, prominent black central stripe and caudal fin flashes. Because of its relatively small size and shoaling habit, it makes an ideal aquarium fish. A group of a dozen with their heads up, swimming together against a moderate current, is an impressive sight. In addition, they are inexpensive, very peaceful, and do not hide during the day like many catfish species. All these factors make them a very attractive proposition for any community or specialist aquarium. They also present an interesting challenge to the serious catfish breeder.

WHAT size?
A medium-sized species, males and females growing to 10cm.

WHAT does it eat?
Naturally feeds on insect larvae; will accept flake, frozen daphnia, cyclops and bloodworm.

WHERE is it from?
Africa: Gabon, River Ogowe. Congo River Basin and Chiloango River.

WHAT does it cost?
★☆☆☆☆
Inexpensive.

▲ *The clean lines of P. debauwi really stand out in this pair of fish.*

HOW do I sex it?
Only possible when the fish have been fully acclimatised and are in top condition. Females have plumper, fuller bodies, especially around the ventral area, and a rounded, short genital papilla.

WHAT kind of tank?
Community or specialist species-only aquarium.

WHAT minimum size tank?
60x30x30cm.

WHAT kind of water?
Top-quality water is essential, soft/medium hard, pH6.5-7.6. This species is sensitive to chemical fluctuations, so carry out regular water changes to maintain the best possible conditions.

HOW warm?
23-26°C.

WHAT decor?
Sand or fine gravel substrate, planted at the sides and rear, leaving plenty of swimming space. Reasonably strong filtration will create the necessary flow to encourage the fish's natural swimming habit.

WHAT area of the tank?
Spends most of the day swimming in the open areas of the aquarium, against the current from the filter, but if conditions are not good it will tend to mope and hide amongst the plants.

HOW many in one tank?
A shoaling species, best kept in groups of at least six.

HOW does it behave?
Very peaceful.

WILL it breed in an aquarium?
No known records of captive breeding. In nature, it spawns during the rainy season.

Pimelodus pictus

Pictus catfish

FISH PROFILE

With a silver body, black spots and elegant lines, the pictus catfish is a striking species. To see it at its active best, provide plenty of swimming space so that it can move around freely. Take care when handling or moving it, as the very sharp, serrated, pectoral fin spines are very easily snagged in nets. They can just as easily prick the skin, which is quite a painful experience that thankfully does not last long.

WHAT size?
Males and females 13.5cm.

WHAT does it eat?
In nature, small fish and insect larvae. Not a fussy eater in the aquarium; readily accepts fish pieces, small strips of beef, flake, tablet and frozen foods.

WHERE is it from?
Peru and Colombia.

WHAT does it cost?
★★☆☆☆
Moderately priced.

HOW do I sex it?
No visual external differences.

WHAT kind of tank?
Community aquarium, or a shoal in a specialist tank.

WHAT minimum size tank?
90x30x30cm.

WHAT kind of water?
Good-quality, soft to medium hard, acid to neutral (pH5.6-7.0).

HOW warm?
22-26°C.

WHAT decor?
Plants, tree roots to create hiding places, with plenty of open areas.

WHAT area of the tank?
All areas.

HOW many in one tank?
Four.

HOW does it behave?
Although considered peaceful, it is best kept with species at least half its size, as small tankmates may be regarded as food.

WILL it breed in an aquarium?
No known records of captive breeding.

▼ Like many Pimelodus *species,* P. pictus *has a sleek appearance and very long barbels, which it uses constantly to feel its way around.*

Scleromystax barbatus

Bearded cory

FISH PROFILE

Because of the striking colours of mature males, this fish has been very popular amongst hobbyists for many years. Formerly known as *Corydoras barbatus*, in 2004 it was returned to its original genus *Scleromystax*, a name taken from the Greek, meaning 'hard bristles'. This is a reference to the odontodes on the sides of the head. Because of pollution in its original habitat, the species has gradually moved up into the headwaters and is becoming harder to find.

▲ *Most male fish are easy to recognise by the bristles on the side of the head.*

WHAT size?
One of the largest species in the family, males reaching 10cm, females 9cm.

WHAT does it eat?
In the wild, insect larvae, aquatic worms and small crustaceans, such as daphnia and cyclops. Offer a variety of tablet, granular, flake or frozen foods. Live bloodworm, tubifex or daphnia will help keep the fish in top condition.

WHERE is it from?
Brazil, State of Rio de Janeiro. The clear water streams of the mountainous regions.

WHAT does it cost?
★★★☆☆
Fairly expensive.

HOW do I sex it?
Males are more colourful, with an almost black head and a body covered with gold spots and streaks. They have longer pectoral and dorsal fins, and odontodes (bristles) on their cheeks. Females have a light tan body and head, covered with dark brown marbling.

WHAT kind of tank?
Community aquarium or specialist breeding tank.

WHAT minimum size tank?
60x30x30cm.

WHAT kind of water?
Clear, good-quality, soft, acid (pH5.5-6.5), but will acclimatise to a wide range of conditions.

HOW warm?
18-21°C.

WHAT decor?
A fine, smooth-grained sand substrate. Pieces of bogwood, large pebbles and plants if desired, but not essential.

WHAT area of the tank?
Bottom-dweller that makes occasional trips to the surface for a gulp of air.

HOW many in one tank?
One pair.

HOW does it behave?
Very peaceful; will not bother other tankmates. Mature males become dominant during the mating season and will squabble over territory.

WILL it breed in an aquarium?
Yes. Given the right conditions, this is relatively easy. The female usually deposits her eggs all together in one place, high up on the side of the tank.

Sorubim lima

Duckbill catfish

FISH PROFILE

This is a member of the group commonly known as shovelnosed catfish. It is a nocturnal species that likes to stay hidden amongst plants and tree roots during the day, its black-white-and-brown-striped colour pattern providing perfect camouflage. It lies with its head pointing downwards, poised and ready to pounce on any unsuspecting fish that passes by. During twilight hours it is more adventurous and, still in the inverted stance, will stalk smaller fishes that are preparing to settle for the night.

WHAT size?
Possibly the smallest of the shovelnosed catfish at 30cm (males and females).

WHAT does it eat?
In nature, a carnivore that predates on smaller fish. Adult fish can be difficult to wean onto proprietary foods, but small specimens are more adaptable and will accept tablet foods and earthworms.

WHERE is it from?
Fairly widespread in the Amazon Basin.

WHAT does it cost?
★★★☆☆
Fairly expensive.

HOW do I sex it?
No visual external differences.

WHAT kind of tank?
Reasonably large community, or single-species aquarium.

WHAT minimum size tank?
90x30x45cm.

WHAT kind of water?
Clean, good-quality, soft to medium hard, slightly acid to slightly alkaline (pH 6.3-7.6), but will accept a wide range of water types.

HOW warm?
23-30°C.

▼ *Sorubim lima, showing why its common name is 'duckbill catfish'.*

WHAT decor?
A sandy substrate planted with broadleaved plants and furnished with tree roots or branches to create hiding places.

WHAT area of the tank?
Likes to hide amongst tree roots or broadleaved plants; not a particularly active species.

HOW many in one tank?
Two.

HOW does it behave?
Although a predator, it is perfectly safe with fishes of equal size or larger.

WILL it breed in an aquarium?
No known records of captive breeding.

Sturisoma panamense

Royal farlowella, royal twig catfish

FISH PROFILE

Although known as the royal farlowella, it does not belong to the genus *Farlowella*. The 'royal' common name stems from its majestic, elegant lines. It is built for life in shallow, fast-moving waters, where its streamlined shape and large flowing fins enable it to navigate easily and hold its position against the fiercest of currents.

WHAT size?
Males and females 20cm.

WHAT does it eat?
Vegetarian by nature; will graze on any algae that forms on the aquarium glass and furnishings. Provide washed lettuce, slices of cucumber or courgette and mashed peas.

WHERE is it from?
Panama.

WHAT does it cost?
★★★☆☆
Fairly expensive. Juveniles (measuring 5-7.5cm) are usually inexpensive (★).

HOW do I sex it?
Males have quite pronounced cheek bristles; females have a slightly more pointed head shape.

WHAT kind of tank?
Community or species-only aquarium.

WHAT minimum size tank?
90x30x45cm.

WHAT kind of water?
Crystal clear, well-filtered and with a strong current, soft, slightly acidic to neutral (pH 6-7).

HOW warm?
25-30°C.

L NUMBER SYSTEM

Many undescribed Loricariid species have been allocated L numbers. With over 300 L numbers available, there are plenty for aquarists to choose, including the beautiful gold nugget (L177) and the snowball pleco (L102).

WHAT decor?
A sandy substrate, with tree roots or branches and broadleaved plants. Delicate leaves may be damaged by the fish's perpetual grazing. Strong lighting to promote algae growth.

WHAT area of the tank?
Will visit and graze on all areas.

HOW many in one tank?
One pair.

HOW does it behave?
Very peaceful.

WILL it breed in an aquarium?
Yes, regularly. After mating is concluded, the male takes full responsibility for looking after the eggs until the fry hatch.

▶ *This is possibly the largest member of the genus and was given the title of 'royal pleco' because of its elegant and regal lines.*

Synodontis flavitaeniatus

FISH PROFILE

With its brown and yellow wavy body pattern, which it maintains throughout its life, this is possibly the most beautiful and one of the most sought-after of all the *Mochocidae* species. It has been a favourite with hobbyists for many years. It is not as secretive as many of its family members, and given the right conditions will happily swim around the aquarium for all to see.

▼ *This relatively easy-to-keep species would make an attractive addition to any community of large fish.*

▼ *A very desirable species, favoured for its unique colour pattern and diurnal habit.*

WHAT size?
Moderately large; males and females 20cm.

WHAT does it eat?
Omnivorous, will eat tablet, granular and frozen foods, live insect larvae, small crustaceans and some algae.

WHERE is it from?
Africa, Zaire, around Pool Malebo (formerly Stanley Pool) near Kinshasa.

WHAT does it cost?
★★★☆☆
Fairly expensive.

HOW do I sex it?
No known visual external differences.

WHAT kind of tank?
Community or specialist aquarium.

WHAT minimum size tank?
90x30x45cm.

WHAT kind of water?
Tolerates a wide range of water conditions, soft to medium hard, pH6.5-8.9.

HOW warm?
23-28°C.

WHAT decor?
A fine gravel substrate, with some well-rooted plants, tree roots or pieces of bogwood to create hiding places and/or some well-chosen rocks. Large-leaved floating plants create the ideal subdued lighting.

WHAT area of the tank?
All areas.

HOW many in one tank?
Two, but more can be accommodated in a larger aquarium.

HOW does it behave?
Like many of this family, it is a little bossy and should be kept with similar-sized species.

WILL it breed in an aquarium?
No known records of captive breeding.

Synodontis multipunctatus
Cuckoo catfish

FISH PROFILE

It is easy to see why *Synodontis multipunctatus* is so popular amongst aquarists, despite its exacting water requirements. Its striking, creamy white body adorned with large sooty-black spots, the large, ever-watchful eyes and its generally peaceful nature, all combined with its unique breeding habits, make it a very desirable fish.

▼ *Perhaps 'Dalmatian' catfish could also describe this species.*

WHAT size?
Males and females up to 15cm.

WHAT does it eat?
Prefers live or frozen foods, but will accept flake, tablet and granular foods. Also known to eat snails.

WHERE is it from?
Africa, Lake Tanganyika.

WHAT does it cost?
★★★☆☆
Fairly expensive.

HOW do I sex it?
Males are a little smaller and have slightly longer pectoral spines. It may be possible to see the short genital papillae in mature males.

WHAT kind of tank?
Most suited to a large community tank with Lake Tanganyika cichlids.

WHAT minimum size tank?
90x30x30cm.

WHAT kind of water?
Good-quality, hard and alkaline (pH7.5-8.5).

HOW warm?
21-26°C.

WHAT decor?
A sandy substrate; some coral sand will help maintain the correct water parameters. To imitate the rocky shoreline of its habitat, provide rock caves and hiding places, with some open areas.

WHAT area of the tank?
Patrols all areas.

HOW many in one tank?
Three or four.

HOW does it behave?
Reasonably peaceful, but may display some territorial behaviour if kept in larger groups.

WILL it breed in an aquarium?
Yes, regularly. The common name 'cuckoo catfish' derives from its habit of darting between spawning cichlids, depositing and fertilising its eggs, and eating as many of the cichlid eggs as it can. The mouthbrooding female cichlid then picks up all the eggs and raises the catfish fry with her own young.

◀ *A head detail showing the feathered barbels of the cuckoo catfish.*

Synodontis nigriventris

Upside-down catfish

FISH PROFILE

Many *Synodontis* species are referred to as 'upside-down catfish', but this one is considered to be the original; it is even recorded in ancient Egyptian wall carvings. Its inverted swimming habit enables it to feed on the mosquito larvae that gather at the surface or under the overhanging leaves of submerged vegetation. It is nocturnal, only venturing out when the light levels drop.

WHAT size?
Males 8-9cm, females 10cm.

WHAT does it eat?
In nature, predominantly insect larvae, especially those of the mosquito. In the aquarium it happily accepts tablet, flake and frozen foods, bloodworm, mosquito larvae and daphnia.

WHERE is it from?
Africa: Zaire. Widespread in slow-moving waters throughout the Congo Basin.

WHAT does it cost?
★☆☆☆☆
Small specimens are usually inexpensive.

HOW do I sex it?
Females are generally larger and plumper than males and usually paler on the belly.

WHAT kind of tank?
Very well suited to a community or species-only aquarium.

WHAT minimum size tank?
60x30x30cm.

WHAT kind of water?
Tolerates a wide range of conditions, but prefers soft, slightly acidic water.

HOW warm?
22-26°C.

WHAT decor?
A well-planted aquarium with broadleaved species that create shady overhangs. Pieces of tree root or bogwood are beneficial. Substrate type is not critical, but should be suitable for healthy plant growth.

WHAT area of the tank?
Prefers to swim upside-down, spending much of its time in this position under overhanging leaves, in the crevices or under the bogwood.

HOW many in one tank?
Group of four.

HOW does it behave?
Somewhat secretive, but very peaceful and good-natured, perfectly suited to any community aquarium.

WILL it breed in an aquarium?
No known records of captive breeding, but said to lay its eggs in a hollow in the substrate, with both parents taking care of the fry.

▲ *Because* Synodontis nigriventris *favours an inverted pose, it has evolved a colour pattern that is darker on the belly than on its back.*

Fish as we imagine them

▶ The name 'barb', meaning 'beard', derives from the whisker-like barbules in the corner of the mouth, but while some species have one or two pairs of these sensory appendages, others lack them. Barbs, egglaying members of the carp family (Cyprinidae) are typically fish-shaped, with no extremes of shape or scalation as found in, for example, catfishes. This lack of specialisation rightly suggests that they are resourceful, active shoalers with a catholic taste in small food items. Their relatively small size (with the exception here of the tinfoil barb) makes them vulnerable to predation. So they are equipped with excellent vision and a good turn of speed to avoid capture. No parental care is shown to eggs or fry. Typical of shoaling cyprinids, hundreds of adhesive or semi-adhesive eggs are scattered in plants or over the substrate after a brief, vigorous courtship.

Price guide

★	£1 or less
★★	£1 – £2
★★★	£3 – £4
★★★★	£4 – £5
★★★★★	£5 +

FISH PROFILE

This fish, a food item where it occurs in the wild, gets its name from the highly reflective silver scales that glisten like kitchen foil under bright light. The large eyes, deeply forked tail and red fins, some edged in black, make this fish an attractive proposition, but only for very large tanks. Do not, therefore, be fooled by cute juveniles. A tendency to dig and uproot plants severely restricts tank decor options.

WHAT size?
Males and females 30cm.

WHAT does it eat?
Flake, frozen and live foods, with plenty of plant matter.

WHERE is it from?
Southeast Asia.

WHAT does it cost?
★★★☆☆
Large specimens are sometimes sold cheaply to free up space in the aquatic shop.

▲ Who would imagine that this juvenile tinfoil barb could grow to a length of 30cm?

Barbodes schwanenfeldi

Tinfoil barb

HOW do I sex it?
Not possible – sexes are identical in size, shape and colour.

WHAT kind of tank?
These avid plant-eaters are very active swimmers. They are usually kept in very large, relatively bare display tanks with other peaceful fishes that outgrow normal community aquariums.

WHAT minimum size tank?
150x60x75cm.

▼ *Deep-bodied tinfoil barbs require correspondingly deep tanks to thrive.*

WHAT kind of water?
Medium hard, slightly acid to slightly alkaline (pH6.5-7.5).

HOW warm?
22-25°C.

WHAT decor?
Tinfoils will uproot and devour plants, so artificial substitutes are a better option. Provide a sandy substrate and avoid rocks with sharp edges, as these fish can be skittish.

WHAT area of the tank?
Middle to top levels.

HOW many in one tank?
As many as space will allow, but no fewer than two.

HOW does it behave?
A peaceful, active shoaler that is always on the move. However, it is not to be trusted with fish smaller than 5cm, which it will regard as live food.

WILL it breed in an aquarium?
No, but is artificially spawned in fish farms.

Barbus arulius

Arulius barb

FISH PROFILE

A slim, medium-sized, rather understated barb that has been in the hobby for more than 150 years. Its colour intensifies with age and the scales show faint iridescence. There are two barely noticeable barbules at the corner of the mouth. Mature males develop extensions to the dorsal fin filaments. An active species, so provide a spacious tank. May eat fine-leaved plants.

WHAT size?
Males and females 12cm.

WHAT does it eat?
Omnivorous: flake; live, freeze-dried or frozen daphnia, mosquito larvae, bloodworm; some plant matter.

WHERE is it from?
South and southeast India.

WHAT does it cost?
★★☆☆☆
Extensively farm-bred, but not quite as cheap as some of the smaller, more popular barbs.

HOW do I sex it?
Males have dorsal fin extensions and spawning tubercles at breeding time, when females are the more rounded.

WHAT kind of tank?
A well-planted community aquarium with similar-sized fish.

WHAT minimum size tank?
75x30x38cm.

WHAT kind of water?
Unfussy, but avoid extremes of pH and hardness.

HOW warm?
20-25ºC.

WHAT decor?
Well-planted tanks with bogwood or rocks, but leave plenty of open swimming areas.

WHAT area of the tank?
Middle to top levels.

HOW many in one tank?
Minimum one pair, but small groups are best.

HOW does it behave?
Peaceful shoaler, though it may eat very small fry and fine-leaved plants.

WILL it breed in an aquarium?
Yes, but a separate spawning tank is required if the eggs are not to be eaten. Around 80 eggs are scattered over plants, hatching in two days.

▲ The dorsal filaments are obvious in the male (top fish).

Barbus conchonius

Rosy barb

FISH PROFILE

A goldfish-like barb with normal and long-finned forms, and many intermediates resulting from mass-farming. This is a long-lived, very hardy and undemanding species. The fish display their best colours at the lower end of the suggested temperature band.

▲ *Rosy barbs prefer water that is on the cool side.*

WHAT size?
Males and females up to 10cm, but usually smaller.

WHAT does it eat?
Omnivorous. The long-finned form may be slow to compete for food, so feed sinking granules as well as flake and freeze-dried items.

WHERE is it from?
Northwest India.

WHAT does it cost?
★☆☆☆☆
Inexpensive. Usually purchased as juveniles.

HOW do I sex it?
Males are redder, with golden scales along the back and a black-edged dorsal fin. Females are greenish gold, and plumper, but in farmed fish both sexes may show red.

WHAT kind of tank?
Community aquarium with similar-sized fish.

WHAT minimum size tank?
75x30x38cm.

WHAT kind of water?
Medium hard, slightly acid to slightly alkaline (pH6.5-7.5).

HOW warm?
18-23°C.

WHAT decor?
Planted tank. The fish shows its colours best over a dark substrate.

WHAT area of the tank?
Middle to top levels.

HOW many in one tank?
Minimum two, but small shoals preferred.

HOW does it behave?
Peaceful; the long-finned form may become a victim of fin-nipping.

WILL it breed in an aquarium?
Yes, possibly the easiest barb to breed – and broods are large (200-300). Use trios of two males and one female in a spawning tank furnished with fine-leaved plants or a spawning mop. Remove the parents as soon as the eggs are deposited.

▲ *A copper, long-finned rosy barb, developed by selective breeding.*

Barbus cumingi
Cuming's barb

FISH PROFILE

A subtly coloured fish which, like the cherry barb, is endangered in the wild. It is deep-bodied, with iridescent scales forming a vignette pattern and two distinct dark vertical bars, one behind the shoulders, the other towards the tail. It is less popular than it used to be, but well worth seeking out.

WHAT size?
Males and females 5cm.

WHAT does it eat?
Live, flake, frozen and some fresh green food.

WHERE is it from?
Sri Lanka.

WHAT does it cost?
★★★☆☆
May have to be ordered specially, although still farmed in fair numbers.

SIMILAR BARBS
Young specimens of Cuming's barb can be easily confused with similar Asian barbs bearing lateral spots, such as *Barbus stoliczanus*, *B. filamentosus* and *B. binotatus*.

▲ *The large eyes are typical of fish that are both hunter and hunted. This is a male.*

HOW do I sex it?
Males are slimmer than females, and more brightly coloured.

WHAT kind of tank?
A mature community tank, not too strongly lit, with plant thickets and open swimming areas.

WHAT minimum size tank?
60x30x30cm.

WHAT kind of water?
Medium hard (does not adapt well to newly set-up tanks). Slightly acid to slightly alkaline (pH6.5-7.5).

HOW warm?
22-27°C.

WHAT decor?
Floating plants to diffuse overhead lighting, plus Java moss and Java fern, and rounded pebbles with some algal covering.

WHAT area of the tank?
Middle to top levels.

HOW many in one tank?
Shoals of four or more.

HOW does it behave?
Assured but unaggressive midwater shoaler.

WILL it breed in an aquarium?
Yes, but requires a separate, well-matured spawning tank with soft water (filtered through peat) and plenty of fine-leaved plants. If the pair do not spawn within three days, remove them, feed plenty of live foods and try again in a week or two.

Barbus everetti

Clown barb

FISH PROFILE

Striking, bluish-black blotches over a warm base colour of iridescent orange give this fish its common name. The long barbules reflect a more bottom-dwelling habit than that of many other barbs. In captivity it can be slow-growing, but it makes an ideal inhabitant for the larger community tank. Will not bother smaller rasboras, tetras, etc.

WHAT size?
Males and females 10cm.

WHAT does it eat?
Accepts all the usual aquarium foods, but prefers some vegetable matter.

WHERE is it from?
Southeast Asia.

WHAT does it cost?
★★★★☆
Usually sold as unsexable juveniles. The relatively high price reflects modest demand rather than difficulty in breeding.

HOW do I sex it?
Males are slimmer than females, and more brightly coloured, although they take longer to mature.

WHAT kind of tank?
A well-filtered and planted, spacious community tank, preferably with a dark substrate to show off the fish's colours. Tankmate selection will be limited, in view of this species' higher-than-average temperature requirements.

WHAT minimum size tank?
90x38x38cm.

WHAT kind of water?
Medium hard, pH7.5-8.5.

HOW warm?
24-29°C.

WHAT decor?
Smooth rocks, bogwood, localised dense thickets of real or artificial plants.

WHAT area of the tank?
Bottom to middle levels.

HOW many in one tank?
As many as space permits.

HOW does it behave?
Despite its size, this is a very peaceful fish and less active than some other barbs.

WILL it breed in an aquarium?
Yes. Place a well-conditioned pair in a mature tank no smaller than 60cm long and furnished with fine-leaved plants or mops. Gradually raise the temperature by 2°C each day to 29°C.

▶ *Barbules, seen prominently here, usually indicate substrate-feeders, but clown barbs swim in midwater too.*

Barbus jae

Jae barb

One of the few African barbs in the hobby, and usually wild-caught, so availability is not constant. Because of their small size and soft-water requirements, they are usually kept either in shoals in a species tank or used as 'dither fish' with dwarf cichlids.

WHAT size?
Males and females 4cm.

WHAT does it eat?
Small live foods (daphnia, cyclops); flake and fine granular foods; freeze-dried mosquito larvae.

WHERE is it from?
Western central Africa.

WHAT does it cost?
★★★★★
The most expensive barb you are likely to encounter.

AFRICAN BARBS
Other sought-after African barbs include dwarf barb (*B. gracilis*) from Nigeria and Cameroon; Congo barb (*B. congicus*) and golden dwarf barb (*B. gelius*) from the Zaire Basin; and four-spot barb (*B. quadripunctatus*) from Tanzania.

HOW do I sex it?
Males are by far the more colourful, with vivid orange/red leading edges to the dorsal, pelvic and anal fins.

WHAT kind of tank?
Species tank.

WHAT minimum size tank?
45x25x25cm.

WHAT kind of water?
Well-matured, very soft (rainwater filtered through peat), acidic (pH5.5-6.0).

HOW warm?
20-26°C.

WHAT decor?
Fine-leaved plants, including some floaters to filter out light, and clumps of *Anubias*.

▲ *Due to their small size, jae barbs can be vulnerable in a community tank. Select tankmates that are not likely to bully, or even eat, them. This is a female.*

WHAT area of the tank?
Middle to top levels.

HOW many in one tank?
As many as you can afford – small groups tend to 'lose' themselves in planted aquariums.

HOW does it behave?
A rather shy shoaling fish, though males will spar among themselves.

WILL it breed in an aquarium?
Yes, but with difficulty. Use well-conditioned trios and place them in a heavily planted spawning tank. The parents are avid egg-eaters.

Barbus nigrofasciatus
Black ruby barb

FISH PROFILE

'Black ruby' describes this barb very well – males are dark, with three indistinct vertical bars, a crimson throat, spangled scales and fins that turn darker at spawning time. Females are yellowish-grey. The dorsal fin of both sexes is strongly convex. It hybridises readily with rosy barbs, so take care to buy a pure strain of fish.

▲ *A male black ruby in full spawning garb.*

WHAT size?
Males and females to 6cm.

WHAT does it eat?
Flake, frozen and live foods.

WHERE is it from?
Sri Lanka.

WHAT does it cost?
★★★☆☆
Usually sold as sexed pairs, hence the relatively high price.

▼ *Females could be mistaken for tiger barbs, but note the lack of banding on the head.*

HOW do I sex it?
Easy – males are slightly larger than females, and have much brighter colours.

WHAT kind of tank?
A well-planted community tank, not too brightly lit and with plenty of plant cover and refuges.

WHAT minimum size tank?
75x38x38cm.

WHAT kind of water?
Medium hard, slightly acid to neutral (pH6.5-7).

HOW warm?
20-26°C.

WHAT decor?
A mixture of fine- and broad-leaved plants, plus bogwood caves. Use spotlights rather than full overhead lighting.

WHAT area of the tank?
Bottom to middle levels.

HOW many in one tank?
Minimum of four (preferably two pairs).

HOW does it behave?
Peaceful with all other fish and an active midwater swimmer, but can be shy if the tank is too well illuminated.

WILL it breed in an aquarium?
Yes. An easy egg-scatterer amid plants, where it lays up to 300 eggs.

91

Barbus oligolepis

Checker barb

FISH PROFILE

An old favourite, first described in 1853 but not seen quite as frequently as in days gone by. Often thought of as a small barb, it seldom grows to more than 10cm in the aquarium, but it can attain 15cm in the wild. Males have silvery blue, strongly vignetted scales, and the crimson fins edged in black appear lit from within.

WHAT size?
Males and females 15cm.

WHAT does it eat?
Live, frozen, flake, granular and green foods.

WHERE is it from?
Indonesia.

WHAT does it cost?
★☆☆☆☆
Inexpensive. Usually sold as unsexable juveniles.

HOW do I sex it?
Males are far more brightly coloured, and slimmer, than females.

WHAT kind of tank?
A mature, well-planted community aquarium with good water circulation, plenty of cover and a dark substrate.

WHAT minimum size tank?
60x30x38cm.

WHAT kind of water?
Soft, acidic (pH6.0-6.5), well-aged.

HOW warm?
20-24°C.

▼ *This is a well-fed male, not a female heavy with eggs.*

WHAT decor?
Not critical, but avoid any calcareous rocks that could raise the pH above 6.5.

WHAT area of the tank?
Middle to top levels.

HOW many in one tank?
The larger the shoal, the more the males will show off their colours to prospective spawning partners.

HOW does it behave?
Active and boisterous with its own kind, but harmless to other tankmates.

WILL it breed in an aquarium?
Yes. Place a pair (selected by strong courtship behaviour in the main tank) in a breeding set-up with soft, aged water at 26°C and they will scatter eggs in surface plants or floating spawning mops.

Barbus tetrazona tetrazona

Tiger barb

FISH PROFILE

An extremely popular, deep-bodied, medium-sized barb, but owing to extensive mass-production it is difficult to find fishes showing crisp banding as seen in the wild. Man-made colour varieties include green, black and albino. Long-finned examples also exist. Fin-nipping is reduced if fish are kept in shoals of six or more.

WHAT size?
Males and females 7cm.

WHAT does it eat?
Flake, frozen and live foods; algae wafers.

WHERE is it from?
Borneo, Indonesia (but almost exclusively tank-bred).

WHAT does it cost?
★★☆☆☆
Mass-produced, but not always to a high standard.

▼ Albino tiger barbs lack any black pigment.

▶ This green strain is known as 'moss'.

HOW do I sex it?
Males are more colourful, while mature females are plumper.

WHAT kind of tank?
Community with other, active fishes. Provide open areas for swimming.

WHAT minimum size tank?
75x30x38cm.

WHAT kind of water?
Unfussy within normal parameters.

HOW warm?
20-26°C.

▲ Tiger barbs are constantly on the move in the aquarium.

WHAT decor?
Shoals look good swimming through stands of *Vallisneria*. Tigers show their best colours over a dark substrate.

WHAT area of the tank?
Middle to top levels.

HOW many in one tank?
Minimum shoal of six.

HOW does it behave?
Boisterous rather than aggressive, but readily fin-nips if not diverted by others of its own kind.

WILL it breed in an aquarium?
Yes – it is a typical egg-scatterer, but make provision to save the eggs from being eaten by the parent fishes.

Barbus ticto var. *'Odessa'*

Odessa barb

FISH PROFILE

Mystery surrounds the origin of this fish which, by general consensus, is simply a colour form of an old aquarium favourite, the ticto barb. Clearly, it did not originate from Odessa, although it may have entered Europe through that port. This would have been feasible, because it can survive down to 14°C.

▼ Like many barbs, this Odessa female shows shoulder and tail spots.

▲ The finnage of mature males is quite resplendent.

WHAT size?
Males and females 10cm.

WHAT does it eat?
Flake, frozen and live foods.

WHERE is it from?
India, Sri Lanka.

WHAT does it cost?
★★★☆☆
The best specimens are now bred in the Czech Republic. Sporadic availability keeps their price up.

HOW do I sex it?
Males have flanks suffused with red, and dark-edged dorsal, pelvic and anal fins with variable numbers of spots. Females are more silvery. Both sexes have dark blotches on the shoulder and caudal peduncle.

WHAT kind of tank?
Well-planted community tank with plenty of open swimming space, and tankmates suited to the lower-than-average temperature for tropical fish. Never keep any barb in an unheated aquarium, however. This is unfair on the fish.

WHAT minimum size tank?
75cmx38x38cm.

WHAT kind of water?
Soft, slightly acid to neutral (pH 6.5-7.0).

HOW warm?
20-23°C.

WHAT decor?
Not critical, but planting is best with temperate, rather than tropical, species, such as *Ludwigia*, *Myriophyllum* and *Azolla*.

WHAT area of the tank?
Middle to top levels.

HOW many in one tank?
These fishes show off their best colours in shoals.

HOW does it behave?
Peaceful and always on the go.

WILL it breed in an aquarium?
Yes. Place a pair in a breeding tank furnished with Java moss or a weighted-down spawning mop, and remove parents immediately the eggs are laid. The fry are large enough to go straight on to newly hatched brineshrimp.

Barbus titteya
Cherry barb

FISH PROFILE

A fish seriously endangered in the wild because of destruction of its natural habitat in Sri Lanka, although its future is assured by captive breeding. A slim, subtly coloured barb with a dark lateral stripe passing through the eye and along the flank, but males in spawning condition practically glow.

WHAT size?
Males and females 5cm.

WHAT does it eat?
Live, flake, frozen and granular food.

WHERE is it from?
Sri Lanka.

▼ *This plump female has been conditioned in readiness for spawning.*

WHAT does it cost?
★★★☆☆
Less popular than it used to be, hence a higher price than you might expect.

HOW do I sex it?
The colour of males in breeding condition reflects the fish's common name. The females are drabber.

WHAT kind of tank?
A well-planted community tank, but choose tankmates carefully in view of its small size.

WHAT minimum size tank?
60x30x30cm.

WHAT kind of water?
Unfussy within normal parameters.

HOW warm?
23-26°C.

WHAT decor?
Rocks, bogwood, some densely planted areas (real or artificial), using fine-leaved plants.

WHAT area of the tank?
Middle to top levels.

HOW many in one tank?
Keep only as pairs unless the tank is 90cm or larger.

HOW does it behave?
Unassuming, and does not naturally form shoals.

WILL it breed in an aquarium?
Yes. Individual eggs are attached to fine-leaved plants by fine filaments. The fry are tiny, and need infusoria or newly hatched brineshrimp as soon as they become free swimming.

▲ *A cherry-red male.*

Naturally gregarious

▶ The characins are one of the largest groups of fishes available in the aquarium hobby and include the popular tetras, many of which are long-standing favourites among fishkeepers. Characins have a unique adaptation known as the 'Weberian apparatus', which connects the hearing organs and the swimbladder, allowing the swimbladder to amplify sounds and provide the fish with an enhanced sense of hearing. Other senses are also more acute in many of the characins and the fish are very aware of changes in their environment. In the wild, this extra sensitivity makes them particularly good at forming shoals, finding food and escaping danger. In the aquarium, take care that vibrations or other stress factors do not shock the fish.

Price guide

★	Up to £2
★★	£2 – £4
★★★	£4 – £8
★★★★	£8 – £12
★★★★★	£12 +

▲ Red phantom tetras are typical small characins, being peaceful and hardy, yet sensitive, shoaling fish.

Almost all characins share similar characteristics, even though at first glance some, such as the neon tetra and the piranha, could not appear more different.

Astyanax mexicanus

Blind cave tetra

FISH PROFILE

Many fishkeepers either love or hate the appearance of these interesting fish. This can be attributed to the unusual absence of eyes, because in its natural cave habitat the fish does not require the power of sight. Despite having no vision, the fish uses highly developed senses, also present in other characins, to locate food and navigate, and it is often the first fish to find food.

WHAT size?
Males and females up to 12cm, normally 8cm.

WHAT does it eat?
Omnivorous. Supplement flake or dried foods with live, frozen or freeze-dried foods.

WHERE is it from?
Originates from Texas, North America, but widely distributed throughout Mexico, North and Central America. Found in sandy and rocky-bottomed pools and backwaters under cave conditions.

WHAT does it cost?
★☆☆☆☆
Easily bred and therefore inexpensive.

HOW do I sex it?
Males are more slender than females.

WHAT kind of tank?
Community aquarium with robust tankmates. Avoid adding delicate species, which may be nipped or disturbed by constant movement.

WHAT minimum size tank?
75x30x38cm.

WHAT kind of water?
Largely undemanding.

HOW warm?
18-25°C. Prefers slightly cooler water and can be kept in an unheated indoor aquarium.

WHAT decor?
No preference, but appreciates swimming space.

WHAT area of the tank?
Middle to bottom levels.

HOW many in one tank?
Keep this lightly shoaling species in a group of three or more.

HOW does it behave?
Peaceful and very active, but may occasionally nip other fish.

WILL it breed in an aquarium?
Yes, breeding is relatively easy and the fry hatch free-swimming after a few days. Breeds more readily at lower temperatures. Interestingly, the fry have fully functional eyes, which regress and become covered as the fry mature.

▲ *A natural lack of visible eyes gives these fish a unique popularity. Blind cave tetras are an unusual addition to the aquarium and attract the attention of all who observe the tank.*

Carnegiella strigata

Marbled hatchetfish

FISH PROFILE

The odd shape of the hatchetfish is due to an enlarged muscle that allows it to jump above the water surface and travel several metres to avoid danger. Because of this well-developed escape response, these fish remain constantly at the surface and a good lid is essential to prevent them jumping from the tank. Hatchetfish are very peaceful and do not bother other fish, making them an ideal addition to a community aquarium.

WHAT size?
Males and females 4cm.

WHAT does it eat?
Offer this surface-feeder a variety of dried foods that will float on the surface. It also enjoys mosquito larvae (black, or blood, worm).

WHERE is it from?
South America: inhabits streams and rivers with overhanging vegetation in the Amazon River Basin.

WHAT does it cost?
★☆☆☆☆ ★★☆☆☆
Availability affects pricing.

HOW do I sex it?
Females have a plumper and more rounded belly.

WHAT kind of tank?
Peaceful community aquarium with planted areas or areas of cover at the surface.

WHAT minimum size tank?
75x45x30cm.

WHAT kind of water?
Prefers soft water, pH5-8.

HOW warm?
24-28°C.

WHAT decor?
Appreciates floating plants, dark substrates and water discoloured by tannins or blackwater extract. Provide hiding places and cover towards the upper part of the aquarium.

▲ *The marbled hatchetfish is a constant surface-dweller, always visible in the aquarium.*

WHAT area of the tank?
Surface-dweller; provide still areas, as well as areas of water flow for the fish to swim against.

HOW many in one tank?
Keep this shoaling fish in a group of at least three.

HOW does it behave?
Peaceful and quiet, staying at the surface and occasionally darting. Can be easily spooked and may jump above the surface.

WILL it breed in an aquarium?
Yes, spawns readily, given a good diet and soft water. It deposits eggs on leaves at the water surface. In a community environment, most eggs will fall and be eaten.

◀ *Black-wing hatchetfish* (Carnegiella marthae).

Gymnocorymbus ternetzi

Black widow tetra

FISH PROFILE

A peaceful shoaling fish that is very hardy and suited to a wide range of water conditions. After about a year, the black colour begins to fade to a washed-out grey, and the fish no longer shoals, preferring its own space. Although very peaceful, the black widow tetra will nip at long-finned fish, such as guppies or Siamese fighting fish (*Betta splendens*).

WHAT size?
Males and females 6cm.

WHAT does it eat?
Omnivorous and opportunistic in nature, feeding on small aquatic animals, seeds and insects. Offer a variety of floating and sinking foods in the aquarium.

WHERE is it from?
South America: Paraguay and Guapore River Basins. Varied river environments.

WHAT does it cost?
★☆☆☆☆ ★★☆☆☆
A long-standing and common aquarium fish that remains fairly constant in price.

HOW do I sex it?
The male's dorsal fin is pointed and narrow, and the anal fin is broader than in the female.

WHAT kind of tank?
Community aquarium with no fancy-finned fish.

WHAT minimum size tank?
60x30x30cm.

WHAT kind of water?
Prefers medium to soft, and acidic water. However, although it originates from soft-water areas, this fish will adapt and live quite happily in harder water.

HOW warm?
20-26°C.

WHAT decor?
The black widow tetra looks best in an aquarium with a darker substrate and plenty of shaded areas. It also appreciates some areas planted with real or artificial vegetation.

WHAT area of the tank?
Middle and upper levels.

HOW many in one tank?
Younger fish will shoal more tightly than adults, but groups of at least four are recommended at any age.

HOW does it behave?
Peaceful and reasonably active. Will shoal in groups. Males occasionally squabble, but this is normal behaviour.

WILL it breed in an aquarium?
Yes. Soft, acidic water and tannins from bogwood or blackwater extract will encourage breeding.

▲ Young fish often show darker markings.

◀ Varieties with long, flowing fins are readily available.

Hasemania nana

Silver tip tetra

FISH PROFILE

A popular and long-standing aquarium species and an excellent community fish, especially for new aquariums. Silver tips are hardy and adaptable and will swim out in the open. Given good water quality and water movement, they develop a solid, attractive appearance. Being confident, open-water swimmers and peaceful by nature, silver tips make good tankmates for more delicate, timid fish, encouraging them to come out into the open.

▲ *The white fin markings draw the eye of the viewer as flashes of movement.*

WHAT size?
Males and females 4cm.

WHAT does it eat?
Flake, frozen and live foods.

WHERE is it from?
South America: small flowing streams and tributaries in Brazil.

WHAT does it cost?
★☆☆☆☆
Readily available and hardy, silver tips are an inexpensive stock aquarium fish.

HOW do I sex it?
Males are more slender, with whiter edging on the anal fin.

WHAT kind of tank?
Peaceful community aquarium.

WHAT minimum size tank?
60x30x30cm.

WHAT kind of water?
Can be kept in soft or hard water, pH 6-8.

HOW warm?
22-28°C.

WHAT decor?
Prefers an open swimming area with some water movement, as well as a few hiding places.

WHAT area of the tank?
Middle; an open-water swimmer.

HOW many in one tank?
Keep in groups of at least four.

HOW does it behave?
Peaceful and moderately active. Swims out in the open, and is more confident in groups. Males will occasionally squabble, but this is normal behaviour. Some specimens may nip at fancy-finned tankmates.

WILL it breed in an aquarium?
Yes, spawning does occur in the home aquarium. The eggs are deposited on the substrate and a separate breeding tank is normally required to raise them successfully.

Hemigrammus bleheri

Rummy-nose tetra

FISH PROFILE

In the right water conditions, the rummy-nose tetra sports a striking red coloration around the head and distinctive horizontal black-and-white tail fin stripes. It is peaceful and can be kept with other small species and some larger, peaceful fish. Keep the fish in groups and provide plenty of hiding places amongst the vegetation.

WHAT size?
Males and females 4cm.

WHAT does it eat?
Flake, freeze-dried and small live or frozen foods.

WHERE is it from?
Rivers and streams with vegetation in South America.

WHAT does it cost?
★☆☆☆☆ ★★☆☆☆
Stock quality affects price.

HOW do I sex it?
Males are thinner; females have a larger belly.

WHAT kind of tank?
Soft-water community aquarium.

WHAT minimum size tank?
75x30x38cm.

WHAT kind of water?
Soft and slightly acidic for optimum health. Although fish may adapt to harder water, their colours will not intensify and their lifespan may be reduced. Can be sensitive to nitrates and chemicals.

HOW warm?
23-27°C.

WHAT decor?
Appreciates planted areas, as well as hiding places and open-water swimming space.

WHAT area of the tank?
Middle levels.

HOW many in one tank?
Keep in groups of five or more.

HOW does it behave?
Peaceful and shoaling. Although it needs hiding places, the fish will spend time out in the open.

WILL it breed in an aquarium?
Yes, but very soft and generally good-quality water conditions are required for spawning. The fish are egg-scatterers and a separate breeding tank is normally required to raise the young successfully.

▲ The red area fades when fish are stressed.

◀ Rummy-nose tetras appear much more natural and pleasing to the eye when kept in large groups.

Hemigrammus erythrozonus

Glowlight tetra

FISH PROFILE

A well-established, popular aquarium fish that fits all the right criteria for a small community fish. Glowlights are hardy, peaceful and small, and add a bright splash of colour. Whilst they can be active, most are quiet shoaling fish that appreciate a few hiding places and mix well with other community or delicate fish. Regular feeds will keep them in top condition, and darker decor will bring out their colour.

WHAT size?
Males 3cm, females 4cm.

WHAT does it eat?
A micro-predator that does best when fed a mix of flake and small frozen foods, such as daphnia or cyclops.

WHERE is it from?
Wild specimens originate from the Essequibo River in South America. Virtually all specimens for sale are captive-bred.

WHAT does it cost?
★☆☆☆☆
Widely available and cheap.

HOW do I sex it?
Males are smaller and more slender than females.

WHAT kind of tank?
Community aquarium with other small peaceful fish. Can be kept with delicate or active fish.

WHAT minimum size tank?
60x30x30cm.

WHAT kind of water?
Natural water conditions are soft and acidic, but most captive-bred fish will adapt to a wider range of conditions. Avoid very hard water.

HOW warm?
24-28°C.

WHAT decor?
Provide hiding places amongst vegetation. Darker substrates and shaded areas will bring out the fishes' colour.

WHAT area of the tank?
Midwater levels.

HOW many in one tank?
Best kept in groups of at least five.

HOW does it behave?
Peaceful and shoaling. The fish stay close together.

WILL it breed in an aquarium?
Yes. Soft, warm water with peat filtration and tannins from bogwood or blackwater extract, along with densely planted areas, will encourage breeding. Glowlights are egg-scatterers and show no parental care.

▲ *Brightly coloured, small and peaceful; glowlights are an excellent fish for the community aquarium.*

Hyphessobrycon anisitsi
Buenos Aires tetra

FISH PROFILE

A hardy and adaptable species that has been readily available for many years. It has a tendency to fin-nip, so as long as you avoid keeping it with long-finned tankmates, it is a bright, peaceful species and ideal for a community aquarium. The fish come from both tropical and cooler waters and do not like water above 26°C. In fact, they can be kept quite happily in unheated indoor tanks, and make good tankmates for other temperate fish.

WHAT size?
Males and females 6cm.

WHAT does it eat?
In the wild, the fish are opportunistic feeders and eat a varied diet, including some plant material. Feed a varied diet of flake, dried, frozen or live foods and include some vegetable-enriched foods.

WHERE is it from?
South America: Parana and Uruguay River Basins. The fish are found in tropical and temperate lakes and ponds.

WHAT does it cost?
★☆☆☆☆
A fish that is good value for money, inexpensive and interesting for the hobbyist.

HOW do I sex it?
Males have brighter red-yellow fins. Females are fuller-bodied.

WHAT kind of tank?
Community aquarium with no long-finned fish.

WHAT minimum size tank?
75x30x38cm. Although small, the fish do like a bit of swimming room in the aquarium.

WHAT kind of water?
Very adaptable to all water conditions.

HOW warm?
18-25°C. Prefers slightly cooler water and can be kept in an unheated aquarium.

WHAT decor?
Undemanding, but appreciates a few hiding spots and plants. Some plants will be nibbled, so hardy varieties are best.

▲ *As the Buenos Aires tetra ages, the body becomes deeper and the markings more defined.*

WHAT area of the tank?
Tends to spend most time in the middle region, but will swim elsewhere.

HOW many in one tank?
Best kept in groups of four or more.

HOW does it behave?
Peaceful and shoaling, can be nippy with long-finned fish and may nibble at delicate plants.

WILL it breed in an aquarium?
Yes, relatively easily, but requires cooler water. The fish spawn amongst vegetation, which can sometimes be removed to a separate raising tank.

Hyphessobrycon eques

Serpae tetra

An active, hardy and brightly coloured fish, well suited to a community aquarium, as long as you take some precautions. Serpaes have a tendency to fin-nip, but providing they are kept in groups, fin-nipping is normally limited to the group, which is perfectly natural. A number of similar-looking tetras are occasionally sold as serpaes. The red colour is often intensified by feeding the fish special foods before they arrive with the dealer, and this sometimes fades a little after you have brought the fish home.

▲ *The red coloration of these attractive fish can be intensified through a varied diet.*

WHAT size?
Males and females 4cm.

WHAT does it eat?
Flake, dried, frozen and live foods. A varied diet will improve colour.

WHERE is it from?
South America: inhabits standing water in streams, pools and small rivers.

WHAT does it cost?
★☆☆☆☆
For a fish with such a bold colour, serpae tetras have a very modest price.

HOW do I sex it?
Males may be more colourful. Females are more rounded and deeper-bodied.

WHAT kind of tank?
Community aquarium with other small fish, but no long-finned species.

WHAT minimum size tank?
60x30x30cm.

WHAT kind of water?
Avoid very hard water.

HOW warm?
22-26°C.

WHAT decor?
Provide hiding places amongst vegetation. Shaded areas and darker decor will bring out the fishes' colour.

WHAT area of the tank?
All areas, but fish tend to favour the middle region.

HOW many in one tank?
Keep in groups of at least five. Serpaes are more peaceful in larger groups.

HOW does it behave?
Serpaes are normally peaceful but have a tendency to nip at other fishes' fins. Avoiding long-finned tankmates and keeping serpaes in groups will reduce this tendency. Squabbles within a group are normal, and serve to reinforce an individual's group status.

WILL it breed in an aquarium?
Yes, spawning does occur in a community aquarium, but raising the young successfully requires a separate breeding tank.

Hyphessobrycon erythrostigma

Bleeding heart tetra

FISH PROFILE

This chunky fish gets its name from the distinctive red dot in the centre of the body. Like other tetras, it is a relatively peaceful shoaling fish that does well in a community aquarium with planted areas. Good water quality and general aquarium conditions are important for long-term health.

WHAT size?
Males and females 6cm.

WHAT does it eat?
Omnivorous; supplement flake or dried food with small live or frozen foods.

WHERE is it from?
South America: Upper Amazon Basin. Normally found in riverbanks or areas of vegetation.

WHAT does it cost?
★☆☆☆☆　★★☆☆☆
Mature stock may cost more than smaller specimens.

HOW do I sex it?
Males have significantly longer dorsal and anal fins.

WHAT kind of tank?
Community aquarium with other peaceful fishes.

WHAT minimum size tank?
60x30x30cm.

WHAT kind of water?
Prefers soft, slightly acidic conditions, but can be kept in water up to pH8, providing it is not too hard.

HOW warm?
24-28°C.

WHAT decor?
Prefers planted and open areas, hiding places and dark substrates.

WHAT area of the tank?
Midwater levels.

HOW many in one tank?
Although a loosely shoaling fish, the bleeding heart can be kept in smaller numbers – a minimum of three.

HOW does it behave?
Peaceful and quiet.

WILL it breed in an aquarium?
Unlikely.

▶ *The bleeding heart tetra often appears larger than other fish of similar length due to its deep body and extended dorsal fin.*

Hyphessobrycon herbertaxelrodi

Black neon tetra

FISH PROFILE

The black neon is a stockier, more robust fish than the captive-bred neon tetra available in the trade. Providing the aquarium is well filtered, with some water flow and shaded areas, these fish are adaptable and hardy. Black neons are peaceful and suited to a community aquarium, although they may nip at fancy-finned fish, such as guppies or Siamese fighters.

WHAT size?
Males and females 4cm.

WHAT does it eat?
Flake, small frozen or live foods.

WHERE is it from?
South America: Paraguay River Basin, but most specimens are now captive-bred.

WHAT does it cost?
★☆☆☆☆
Inexpensive starter fish.

HOW do I sex it?
Males are slimmer, females more rounded.

WHAT kind of tank?
Community with other small fish.

WHAT minimum size tank?
60x30x30cm.

WHAT kind of water?
Adaptable, but does best in soft to medium-hard water.

HOW warm?
24-27°C.

WHAT decor?
Prefers a few planted areas and/or shaded spots. Darker substrates or a densely aquascaped tank will bring out the fishes' colour.

WHAT area of the tank?
All areas; sometimes rests just above the substrate.

HOW many in one tank?
Keep in groups of at least five.

HOW does it behave?
Peaceful and shoaling; the fish normally stay together, sometimes hovering in the same spot.

WILL it breed in an aquarium?
Yes. A separate tank is normally required, with a densely planted area and soft, acidic water.

▼ *Black neons, like many bold-coloured fish, look their best in natural surroundings and shaded areas.*

Leporinus fasciatus
Banded leporinus

FISH PROFILE

This strikingly patterned fish belongs to the headstander group, although it only occasionally displays the distinctive 'head-down' resting position. Bear in mind its eventual size before buying it. There are several subspecies with slight variations in size and pattern, and these are often sold under the same name. The banded leporinus is a good addition to a larger aquarium with other good-sized, robust and peaceful fishes.

▼ Bright patterning makes these fish a target for impulse buying, but they quickly outgrow small tanks.

WHAT size?
Males and females up to 30cm.

WHAT does it eat?
Feed the young on vegetable- or algae-based flakes, and larger specimens on pellets and algae wafers, plus lettuce leaves or plants. Will also take frozen or live foods.

WHERE is it from?
Central South America: usually in fast-flowing waters with rocky areas.

WHAT does it cost?
★★☆☆☆   ★★★★★
Prices vary depending on supply and size.

HOW do I sex it?
No known visual external differences.

WHAT kind of tank?
Community aquarium with sizeable and robust tankmates.

WHAT minimum size tank?
120x45x45cm.

WHAT kind of water?
In the wild, acidic to neutral, but the fish adapt easily to a wide range of conditions.

HOW warm?
22-26°C.

WHAT decor?
Large pieces of bogwood and rocks, plus a sandy substrate will best recreate the natural habitat. Provide areas of strong flow and good filtration.

WHAT area of the tank?
Tends to stay around the middle and lower regions.

HOW many in one tank?
Some specimens can be troublesome towards tankmates of the same species, so best kept either singly or in groups.

HOW does it behave?
Generally peaceful, although some specimens can be prone to nipping tankmates. Active and interesting in the right aquarium.

WILL it breed in an aquarium?
Unlikely; in the wild, spawning takes place in response to environmental changes.

Metynnis argenteus

Silver dollar

FISH PROFILE

The silver dollar is closely related to the piranha, but is almost exclusively vegetarian. It can be quite nervous and timid, especially when young, so keep it in an aquarium where it is unlikely to be unduly frightened by outside activity. The round body gives it a strong presence in the aquarium, and a group will make excellent tankmates for other large peaceful fish and even some larger cichlids.

WHAT size?
15cm, although it appears larger due to the round shape.

WHAT does it eat?
Naturally feeds almost exclusively on vegetation and seeds, and this diet should be reflected in the aquarium. Pellet foods are best for adult fish, but all specimens will take herbivorous flake, algae wafers, lettuce, cucumber and plant matter.

WHERE is it from?
South America: found in rivers with vegetation both above and below the water.

WHAT does it cost?
★★☆☆☆
Price depends on size and maturity. Young fish (rated here) are relatively cheap but fully grown adults can vary in price considerably.

HOW do I sex it?
Males have a slightly larger and more colourful anal fin.

WHAT kind of tank?
Community with other large and relatively peaceful fish.

WHAT minimum size tank?
120x45x45cm.

WHAT kind of water?
Acidic to neutral in the wild, but will adapt to a wide range of conditions.

HOW warm?
24-28°C.

▼ *Although piranha-like in appearance, silver dollars are timid, peaceful vegetarians.*

WHAT decor?
Undemanding, but appreciates a few large hiding places under wood or rocks.

WHAT area of the tank?
Middle and lower levels.

HOW many in one tank?
Best kept in groups of at least four.

HOW does it behave?
Peaceful and active, although it can be nervous and easily spooked.

WILL it breed in an aquarium?
Yes, but requires soft water and a large aquarium. The male's colour will intensify and pattern variations may appear when he is in spawning condition.

Nannostomus beckfordi
Golden pencilfish

FISH PROFILE

The golden pencilfish is one of the most adaptable of the pencilfish family, but unlike other species that may require soft acidic water, this one can be kept in moderately hard water. The red body coloration will intensify in the right environment and established specimens look much more attractive than when they are first purchased. Good water quality is essential, and because the fish are timid, they should not be mixed with boisterous species.

WHAT size?
Males and females 6cm.

WHAT does it eat?
Flake and/or dried foods, supplemented with small frozen or live foods.

WHERE is it from?
South America: Guyana, found in vegetated waters.

WHAT does it cost?
★☆☆☆☆ ★★☆☆☆
Excellent value for money for such a well-marked and unique fish. Prices are quite similar for young and mature specimens; any variations are mainly caused by suppliers and availability of stock.

HOW do I sex it?
The male has a slender body with white tips on the fins.

WHAT kind of tank?
Community with other peaceful and quiet fishes. Ideal for small planted aquariums.

WHAT minimum size tank?
60x30x30cm.

WHAT kind of water?
Most pencilfish require soft water, although this species will adapt to most conditions.

HOW warm?
24-26°C.

▼ *The phrase 'small but beautiful' is an accurate description of these stunning little fish.*

WHAT decor?
Provide heavily vegetated areas and a dark substrate.

WHAT area of the tank?
Middle and upper levels; the fish will take up position depending on the height of the decor or planting.

HOW many in one tank?
Groups of six or more are best.

HOW does it behave?
Very peaceful, relatively quiet and slow-moving. Males may display to each other.

WILL it breed in an aquarium?
Yes, warmer water will encourage spawning. Eggs are either scattered or deposited, but there is no parental care.

Nematobrycon palmeri

Emperor tetra

The emperor tetra is an attractively coloured fish that will do well in a planted community of other small, peaceful fishes. Good water conditions and a varied diet are essential for long-term health and good colour. A planted environment, or a darker tank with plenty of hiding places, is preferable. A few colour forms are available, including a black variety, although the natural purple-black form is arguably the best-looking. A hardy and long-lived fish in the right environment.

Female

Male

▲ *Once established, male emperors will show stunning markings and intense coloration.*

WHAT size?
Males and females 5cm.

WHAT does it eat?
A varied diet that includes flake, dried foods and small frozen or live foods.

WHERE is it from?
South America: vegetated waters in Colombia.

WHAT does it cost?
★☆☆☆☆   ★★☆☆☆
Supplies of this fish are not as reliable as they used to be, which may cause some variations in price.

HOW do I sex it?
Males have longer fins and a humped back.

WHAT kind of tank?
Community aquarium with other similar-sized fish. Avoid very boisterous tankmates.

WHAT minimum size tank?
60x30x30cm.

WHAT kind of water?
Natural water conditions are soft and acidic, but the fish will adapt to harder water.

HOW warm?
24-28°C.

WHAT decor?
Plenty of densely planted areas and dark retreats.

WHAT area of the tank?
Middle; providing plenty of retreats are available, the fish will come out often.

HOW many in one tank?
Groups of four or more. Can be kept in smaller numbers if only one male is present.

HOW does it behave?
Peaceful and quiet, although males will occasionally squabble. These fish are at their best in a well-planted tank.

WILL it breed in an aquarium?
Not very often. Warm, soft water is required. The parents often eat the eggs.

Paracheirodon axelrodi

Cardinal tetra

FISH PROFILE

The cardinal tetra can be distinguished from the neon tetra by the red and blue bars that extend along the whole body in the cardinal. In recent years, cardinals have become a more popular alternative to the neon, and good specimens can be hardier than some weak stocks of neons. These fish look best when kept in large groups of 10 to 20 or more, space permitting. Given the right conditions, these fish are a perfect addition to a peaceful community aquarium.

WHAT size?
Males and females 5cm.

WHAT does it eat?
Flake, dried, small frozen or live foods.

WHERE is it from?
South America: the fish stay in large shoals of hundreds in open, but shaded, waters.

WHAT does it cost?
★☆☆☆☆ ★★☆☆☆
Captive breeding means lower prices.

HOW do I sex it?
Male are slender, while females are more rounded.

WHAT kind of tank?
Community aquarium.

WHAT minimum size tank?
60x30x30cm.

WHAT kind of water?
Soft, slightly acidic water is essential for long-term health. Although tank-bred fish acclimatised to hard water are available, they often have a shorter lifespan if kept in hard water.

HOW warm?
24-28°C.

WHAT decor?
Planted areas and open swimming space. Cardinals do not like a brightly lit aquarium, so provide some shaded retreats.

WHAT area of the tank?
Middle levels.

HOW many in one tank?
Cardinals must be kept in groups – the bigger the better. Keep a shoal of at least six.

HOW does it behave?
Peaceful, shoaling; will stay near other cardinals.

WILL it breed in an aquarium?
Yes, but soft, acidic water and densely planted areas are essential. The fish are egg-scatterers and a separate breeding tank is required to raise the young.

◀ Cardinals were once considered more difficult but better-looking fish than neons, but today, captive-bred specimens are suited to the general community aquarium.

Paracheirodon innesi

Neon tetra

FISH PROFILE

The neon tetra is arguably the best-known and most popular tropical aquarium fish. Because of this, most specimens are mass-bred and now show signs of weakness associated with extensive breeding. Neons require good water conditions and an established aquarium, and are not a good starter fish. However, once established, they prove hardy and robust, and will live for several years in a favourable environment. For the best visual effect, keep a large group together. Avoid tankmates large enough to eat these small tetras and only keep them with other peaceful species.

WHAT size?
Males and females 4cm.

WHAT does it eat?
Flake, dried, frozen and live foods.

WHERE is it from?
South America: East Peru. Inhabits streams and vegetated rivers. Virtually all neons in the trade are captive-bred.

WHAT does it cost?
★☆☆☆☆
Cheap, but larger specimens are worth paying extra for.

▶ *Check for good colour and body shape to ensure that you buy healthy fish.*

HOW do I sex it?
Males are slender, while females are more rounded.

WHAT kind of tank?
Community with other small fish.

WHAT minimum size tank?
60x30x30cm.

WHAT kind of water?
Natural water conditions are soft and acid, but fish will adapt to hard water.

HOW warm?
24-26°C. Wild fish can tolerate cooler water, but specimens sold in the trade are virtually all tank-bred and must be kept in a heated aquarium.

WHAT decor?
Provide planted areas and dark retreats. Fish also appreciate darker substrates.

WHAT area of the tank?
Middle and lower levels.

HOW many in one tank?
Must be kept in groups of at least five.

HOW does it behave?
Peaceful and quiet.

WILL it breed in an aquarium?
Yes. Soft, acidic water and patches of dense vegetation will encourage spawning.

In recent years, many variations of the neon have appeared in the hobby, offering the fishkeeper a good choice. These are called 'brilliant diamond'.

Phenacogrammus interruptus

Congo tetra

FISH PROFILE

Congo tetras are excellent shoaling fish for larger tanks and communities of medium-sized fish. Mature males can be very colourful, with long, ragged, flowing fins. Good water quality and low nitrates are essential, as well as open swimming areas and hiding places. The iridescent sheen is best seen against darker substrates and decor. Although Congo tetras may nibble at delicate plants, they rarely do much damage and can be kept in planted tanks. They are easily spooked, so site the aquarium in a quiet spot with little external disruption.

WHAT size?
Males 8cm, females 6cm.

WHAT does it eat?
Flake, dried food, small pellets, live and frozen foods. Will also eat some vegetable matter, including delicate plants.

WHERE is it from?
Africa: open and flowing waters in the Zaire River Basin.

WHAT does it cost?
★★☆☆☆
Young are relatively expensive but seem good value when mature. Larger fish cost more.

HOW do I sex it?
Males are larger, more brightly coloured and have longer finnage.

WHAT kind of tank?
Community of medium-sized fishes. Avoid keeping them with delicate species.

WHAT minimum size tank?
90x45x45cm.

WHAT kind of water?
Prefers soft water, but will adapt to harder conditions.

HOW warm?
23-26°C.

WHAT decor?
Shaded areas and darker substrates will show off the fish's colours best. Provide hiding spots and open spaces.

WHAT area of the tank?
Congo tetras like to swim in the open in the middle-upper regions.

HOW many in one tank?
Congos are shoaling fish and should be kept in groups of at least five.

HOW does it behave?
Peaceful and active; shoals in open areas. Congos can be timid, so avoid keeping them with aggressive tankmates.

WILL it breed in an aquarium?
Unlikely but possible. Provide a separate breeding tank.

◄ ▼ An established male Congo tetra (below) is a noticeable presence in the aquarium. A female fish is shown at left.

Pristella maxillaris

X-ray tetra

FISH PROFILE

The distinctive yellow, black and white markings on the fins give this fish an understated appeal in the aquarium. Being robust, adaptable and peaceful, X-rays make excellent community fish. For best visual effect and good health, the aquarium should have partially shaded areas and patches of dense vegetation.

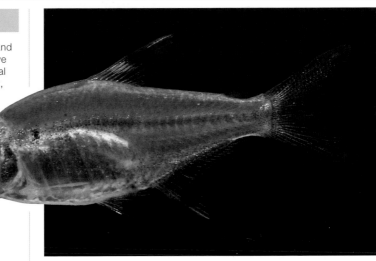

WHAT size?
Males and females 5cm.

WHAT does it eat?
Omnivorous; feeds on small aquatic animals in the wild. Offer a varied diet of flake, dried foods and small live or frozen foods.

WHERE is it from?
South America: found in calm, vegetated waters. Virtually all specimens offered for sale are captive-bred.

WHAT does it cost?
★☆☆☆☆
Easily bred in large numbers and readily available, these fish cost little, which may play a part in their continued popularity in the hobby.

▲ *The popular X-ray tetra is a good choice for the community aquarium.*

HOW do I sex it?
Males are slender and females have a more rounded belly.

WHAT kind of tank?
Community with other small peaceful fish.

WHAT minimum size tank?
60x30x30cm.

WHAT kind of water?
X-Rays are undemanding of water conditions and will do well in hard or soft water, although soft water will bring out their best colours. Can also be kept in brackish water.

HOW warm?
24-28°C.

WHAT decor?
A few densely planted areas, as well as shaded spots and a darker substrate, are ideal.

WHAT area of the tank?
Middle region.

HOW many in one tank?
Keep in groups of five or more.

HOW does it behave?
Peaceful and shoaling; may occasionally nip very fancy-finned fish.

WILL it breed in an aquarium?
Yes, spawns easily in the aquarium, producing several hundred eggs. In a community tank the eggs are usually eaten, unless removed to a separate raising tank.

Pygocentrus nattereri

Red-bellied piranha

FISH PROFILE

Contrary to popular opinion, piranhas are actually very timid fish when kept in smaller numbers in the aquarium, and younger specimens are easily spooked. Their renowned bloodthirsty behaviour only applies to the huge shoals found in the wild, and is greatly exaggerated. However, given their shy nature and potential size, think carefully before purchasing these fish.

WHAT size?
25cm in the aquarium, larger in the wild.

WHAT does it eat?
Frozen meaty foods, including cockles, mussels and fish, or larger live foods, such as shrimps, should make up half the diet. The other half should consist of dried pellet foods. Dried preparations are important, since they provide vitamins and minerals that may be lacking in other foods.

WHERE is it from?
South America: Amazon River Basin.

WHAT does it cost?
★★☆☆☆ ★★★☆☆
Price may vary considerably depending on specimen size, maturity and supplier.

HOW do I sex it?
Mature males are a gold-silver colour with a more pronounced red area, females are more yellow.

WHAT kind of tank?
Best kept in a species tank or with other large, robust fishes.

WHAT minimum size tank?
150x60x60cm.

WHAT kind of water?
Undemanding, but avoid very hard, alkaline water.

HOW warm?
22-28°C.

WHAT decor?
Provide hiding spots amongst large pieces of bogwood. Robust plants are safe, but more delicate plants may be eaten.

WHAT area of the tank?
Middle region.

▲ *Young male already showing adult coloration.*

HOW many in one tank?
Best housed in groups of at least four, but keep an eye out for weaker individuals, which may need to be removed if picked on.

HOW does it behave?
Scatty when young, slow-moving and timid when mature. May on occasion take bites out of fellow tankmates, but with good care these wounds will heal.

WILL it breed in an aquarium?
Yes. Breeding is possible, but requires a very large aquarium. Spawning usually takes place after water changes, and the parents will protect the young.

Thayeria boehlkei

Penguin tetra

FISH PROFILE

The penguin tetra's prominent black line and unusual swimming/resting motion can be eye catching, and give it a strong presence amongst similar-sized tankmates. Good water quality is essential, as these fish are sensitive to pollutants and chemicals. Otherwise, they are relatively easy to care for and make a good addition to a community aquarium of similar-sized fishes.

WHAT size?
Males and females 6cm.

WHAT does it eat?
Flake, live, freeze-dried and frozen foods.

WHERE is it from?
South America: Upper Amazon River Basin. Usually found in densely vegetated waters, often with reeds, suggesting that their distinctive markings are partly camouflage.

WHAT does it cost?
★☆☆☆☆ ★★☆☆☆
Normally inexpensive. Bigger specimens may have a higher price but are more robust and easier to adapt to aquarium life.

HOW do I sex it?
Can be difficult to sex, but females generally have a larger stomach.

WHAT kind of tank?
Community aquarium.

WHAT minimum size tank?
60x30x30cm.

WHAT kind of water?
Penguin tetras come from a wide range of natural conditions and will adapt to most aquariums.

HOW warm?
22-28°C.

WHAT decor?
Appreciates densely vegetated areas and hiding places. The decor should reach up to the surface in some areas.

WHAT area of the tank?
Middle to upper levels.

HOW many in one tank?
Keep in groups of at least four.

HOW does it behave?
Peaceful and quiet. The fish will stay in close groups and 'hover' in preferred areas of the tank.

WILL it breed in an aquarium?
Yes, good water conditions and a favourable environment will encourage breeding. The fish can produce a large number of eggs, although these are usually eaten in a community aquarium.

◀ *The effect of the strong 'hockey stick' markings and head-up swimming style are enhanced when the fish are kept in larger groups.*

Dazzling jewels

▶ Killifish are among the most beautifully coloured aquarium fish. Many species are quite specialised and rarely found in shops, but as a member of a specialist society you will have the opportunity to buy them, plus access to the expertise to help you enjoy them. Killifish, also known as egglaying toothcarps, live in a wide range of habitats from Asia and Africa to North and South America. Most are found in freshwater, but some live in coastal 'brackish' waters and coastal marine areas. Many species that live in areas prone to marked seasonal changes and droughts are annual fish that hatch, mature, spawn and die within a relatively short period. They lay their eggs in the substrate, where they 'rest' before hatching when the following year's rain falls.

Price guide

★	Up to £2
★★	£2 – 3.50
★★★	£5 – 10
★★★★	£10 – 15
★★★★★	£20 – 30

Others with a longer lifespan lay their eggs in fine-leaved plants and peat fibres. Both types can be bred in the aquarium.

Its striking appearance makes the lyretail one of the best-known killifish. Its original colour was dark brown with white extensions, which explains why it was also called the chocolate australe. Over time, an orange form appeared, which proved popular in the hobby due to its vivid 'gold' colour.

WHAT size?
Males 5.5cm, females 5cm.

WHAT does it eat?
Flake food, brineshrimp, frozen and live daphnia and bloodworm.

WHERE is it from?
West Africa: parts of Gabon, Cameroon and Zaire.

WHAT does it cost?
★★★☆☆
Price reflects the quality of the fish, usually sold in pairs. The stronger its coloration, the more expensive the fish.

Aphyosemion australe

Lyretail killifish

HOW do I sex it?
Males are more colourful and have long, white extensions to the tips of the caudal, dorsal and anal fins. Females are slightly smaller, less colourful and have no extensions to the tips of the fins.

WHAT kind of tank?
A well-planted community aquarium with fish of a similar size or smaller, such as small gouramis, tetras and corydoras catfish. Pairs are best kept on their own in a species tank, particularly if you wish to breed them.

WHAT minimum size tank?
25x20x20cm for one pair or a trio of one male and two females.

WHAT kind of water?
These fish cope well with a wide-ranging pH but prefer pH5.5-7, soft to medium-hard water.

HOW warm?
21-25.5°C.

WHAT decor?
Well-planted tanks with dense vegetation and plenty of hiding places. Floating plants provide additional refuges, as well as safe areas for fry.

WHAT area of the tank?
Middle and upper levels.

HOW many in one tank?
A trio of two females to one male is best in a species-only tank. In a larger community aquarium, two or three pairs will live together happily, depending on the size of the tank.

HOW does it behave?
Relatively peaceful. Males readily engage in flirtatious behaviour with the females, producing a dazzling display of colour in the tank.

WILL it breed in an aquarium?
Yes, hiding the eggs in fine-leaved plants such as *Myriophyllum* and Java moss or spawning mops. Once hatched, fry will find cover among floating plants. In a species tank, parents, eggs and fry can be left together. Although some eggs and fry will inevitably be eaten by the parents, fry left in the same tank as their parents appear to grow better. However, killifish specialists often remove the eggs and rear them in a separate tank to improve the numbers of fry raised. First fry foods include infusoria, brineshrimp and microworm.

▲ *A male gold lyretail killifish The vibrant colours and erect finnage suggest that he is displaying to a potential mate.*

SPAWNING MOPS
If you wish to breed killifish, spawning mops are an extremely useful way of collecting the eggs. These are easy to make by winding several strands of wool around a 15-20cm piece of cardboard or a small book. Slip the loops of wool off the cardboard and secure them about 2.5cm from the top around a cork or small piece of floating material. Cutting the opposite end of the loop creates a mop effect, which can then be floated in the tank.

Aplocheilichthys normani

Norman's lampeye

FISH PROFILE

A small fish with an almost transparent, silvery grey body and bright black eyes. These have an iridescent blue upper edge that shines like a torchlight in the aquarium, particularly when the lights are off. Young adults develop a golden casting over the upper part of the body and fins. To see these extremely peaceful fish at their best, keep them in a large shoal of 30 or more, if possible.

WHAT size?
Males 4cm, females 3.8cm.

WHAT does it eat?
Brineshrimp, daphnia and cyclops, plus small flake, freeze-dried and frozen foods.

WHERE is it from?
Africa: in Senegal, Sudan and Nigeria.

WHAT does it cost?
★☆☆☆☆
Relatively cheap to buy individually. Keeping a shoal is inexpensive.

HOW do I sex it?
Males have slightly longer dorsal and anal fins, while the female's fins are more rounded.

WHAT kind of tank?
A shoal will live happily in a community aquarium, along with other small fish that grow no larger than 5cm, such as the rocket panchax, *Rasbora maculata*, Surinam blue rivulus, sparkling gourami, *Corydoras pumilis*, cardinal tetra, black neon and, of course, neon tetra.

WHAT minimum size tank?
Tank size will vary depending on the fish you intend to keep together, but generally speaking a tank measuring 60x30x30cm will provide a good home for a shoal of 30 fish.

WHAT kind of water?
Tolerates dechlorinated tapwater of about 6.5-7 pH and most ranges of hardness. Requires no special water conditions, but as with all fish, this species benefits from frequent water changes.

HOW warm?
22-26°C.

WHAT decor?
To create a really stunning aquarium, use black gravel and soft green plants, such as *Cabomba, Anubias, Echinodorus* (Amazon sword), *Cryptocoryne* and *Vallisneria*. A shoal of neon tetras swimming in the low to middle area of the tank and a shoal of Norman's lampeyes, which occupy the middle to top levels, will make an impressive sight!

WHAT area of the tank?
A shoal will occupy the top and upper middle of the aquarium.

HOW many in one tank?
In large shoals of at least 30, these fish not only look good, but also appear more comfortable.

HOW does it behave?
An incredibly peaceful species that rarely displays aggressive tendencies. Like most fish that occupy the upper regions of the aquarium, they have been known to jump, so a well-fitting aquarium lid is essential.

WILL it breed in an aquarium?
Yes, the fish will breed in a community aquarium, usually amongst the fine-leaved plants in the upper half of the tank. Eggs are deposited on the leaves and those that have been fertilised will hatch and the fry take their chances amongst the other fish. If you decide to harvest the eggs, keep them in a smaller aquarium until they hatch. Feed the fry in the same way as *Rivulus xiphidus* (see page 129).

▼ With its bright shining eyes, this male lampeye lives up to its common name.

Aplocheilus lineatus
Sparkling panchax

FISH PROFILE

A very easy-to-keep, top-swimming fish, with a large wide mouth that appears to be permanently smiling! There are several colour varieties, including a spectacular yellow form known as the golden wonder. A number of the surface swimming killifish, including the sparkling panchax, have developed a shiny scale on the top of their heads that attracts insects. Flies and insects tempted by the shiny scale quickly find themselves the meal of the day.

WHAT size?
Males about 9cm, females approximately 10cm.

WHAT does it eat?
Flake and granular food, live and frozen bloodworm, daphnia, gnat and mosquito larvae, glassworm. Not fussy eaters.

WHERE is it from?
India and throughout Asia.

WHAT does it cost?
★★☆☆☆
Not expensive for a colourful surface swimmer.

HOW do I sex it?
Males are more colourful and have longer fins. Females are slightly bigger and stockier.

WHAT kind of tank?
Makes a good neighbour in the community tank if housed with fish of a similar size or larger.

WHAT minimum size tank?
60x30x30cm.

WHAT kind of water?
Normal, dechlorinated tapwater. Tolerates most water conditions.

HOW warm?
21-28°C.

WHAT decor?
Well-planted tank with plenty of floating vegetation.

WHAT area of the tank?
Likes to hide in floating plants close to the water surface, ready to snatch greedily at any food that drops into the tank.

▲ *The golden wonder is a superb yellow variety with a sparkling 'smile'.*

HOW many in one tank?
Three females to one male in a minimum size tank of 60x30x30cm.

HOW does it behave?
A voracious feeder that will bully smaller fish at mealtimes to ensure that it takes the lion's share of food. Lives happily in the upper part of the aquarium, providing colour and movement amongst the floating plants.

WILL it breed in an aquarium?
Yes, spawns readily. The eggs are caught up in the roots of floating plants or spawning mops. To prevent predation, remove spawning mops to a separate tank so that the eggs can hatch safely. First foods include microworm and newly hatched brineshrimp. Powdered fry foods are an alternative.

Aplocheilus panchax

Blue panchax

FISH PROFILE

As a result of its broad distribution, there is a wide colour variation in this lively yet relatively peaceful fish. Well tolerated in a community tank by other fish of equal size or larger, but can have a tendency to see other males of its own kind as rivals, and may bully fish smaller than itself.

WHAT size?
Males and females 8cm.

WHAT does it eat?
Accepts a wide range of foods, including micro-flake (not to be confused with fry food) and granular food; frozen and freeze-dried food, daphnia, cyclops, mosquito larvae, small bloodworm and whiteworm.

WHERE is it from?
Southern India, Burma, Thailand, Malaysia, Sumatra, Borneo, Java and smaller islands of the Indo-Australian Archipelago.

WHAT does it cost?
★★☆☆☆
This fish is an inexpensive addition to the aquarium.

INFUSORIA
Infusoria are microscopic organisms that live in water and feed on rotting plant matter. They form an ideal first food for tiny fry fishes.

▲ *The elegant blue panchax is a top-swimming fish and an Olympic jumper!*

HOW do I sex it?
Males are more colourful, especially in the fins. The duller females are more rounded.

WHAT kind of tank?
Species tank or community aquarium.

WHAT minimum size tank?
Species tank for one male and two females: 25x15x15cm. Community tank: size depends on the type and number of other fish to be housed with the blue panchax, but larger than a species tank.

WHAT kind of water?
Dechlorinated tapwater, pH7, but water conditions are not critical, as these fish will tolerate most types.

HOW warm?
20-28°C.

WHAT decor?
A well-planted tank that includes Java fern, *Anubias* species and Java moss. Tanks must also have cover provided by floating plants, such as Indian fern *(Ceratopteris thalictroides* and *C. pteridoides)*.

WHAT area of the tank?
Middle, but fish do tend to spend much of their time at the surface, looking for food amongst the floating plants.

HOW many in one tank?
A ratio of three to four females to one male. As males initiate spawning, this ratio prevents the females being excessively pestered. Apply the same ratio when keeping larger groups of these fish.

HOW does it behave?
A relatively peaceful top-swimming fish, but an excellent jumper. A tight-fitting aquarium lid is essential. Lives comfortably with fish of a similar size or larger, such as those with whom it would naturally share its habitat, including *Trichogaster, Colisa* and *Trichopsis* spp., mouthbrooding bettas and rasboras.

WILL it breed in an aquarium?
Yes. Fish spawn in mops or fine-leaved plants. Depending on the water temperature, eggs will hatch in 10-14 days. If not eaten by the parents, fry are easy to raise. Feed them infusoria, brineshrimp and other suitable fry foods.

Australobias nigripinnis

Argentine pearlfish

FISH PROFILE

This stunning annual fish once belonged to the genus *Cynolebias* and has been very popular for many years. Males are extremely striking, having a navy blue to black body and fins, peppered with bright blue-green spots and a bright blue-green band running across the dorsal fin. Given their lively and often aggressive nature, these killies require a species tank.

WHAT size?
Males 5cm, females 4cm.

WHAT does it eat?
Bloodworm, daphnia, mosquito larvae, glassworm, whiteworm. Sometimes accepts frozen foods.

WHERE is it from?
Argentina, parts of southern Brazil and Uruguay.

WHAT does it cost?
★★★★☆ ★★★★★
Not often available in the shops, but could be obtained from a specialist killifish group. The price of a pair reflects the limited availability.

HOW do I sex it?
Males are brightly coloured, while the smaller females tend to be brown-grey.

WHAT kind of tank?
Species tank only.

WHAT minimum size tank?
30x20x15cm for one pair.

WHAT kind of water?
Soft, slightly acid water, pI I6, is best. Benefits from regular water changes.

HOW warm?
20-22°C.

WHAT decor?
Peat fibre on the base of a lightly planted tank that has space for free swimming.

WHAT area of the tank?
Midwater to bottom swimmer.

HOW many in one tank?
One pair per species tank.

HOW does it behave?
A lively, often aggressive killifish.

WILL it breed in an aquarium?
Yes. The most successful method is to set up a species tank with peat fibre on the base to a depth of 5cm and several hiding places for the female. The spawning embrace takes place in the peat fibre and the eggs are deposited there. Remove the peat with the eggs, squeeze out most of the water and place it in a plastic bag to 'rest'. This process simulates what would happen in nature and the eggs may remain viable in this state for up to two years. When you wish the eggs to hatch, place the peat in a tank with fresh, soft water and hatching will begin. If it does not occur after the first 'wetting', place the squeezed-out peat into a plastic bag for a further rest, then try again.

▶ *In spite of her duller appearance, the smaller female is a magnet for the stunning male.*

▲ *Males become more striking in colour as they mature and make the most of a very short lifespan.*

Epiplatys annulatus

Rocket panchax

This small, colourful, very active top swimmer gets its common name from its elongated rocket shape, with a red 'flame' burning from the centre of the caudal fin. The caudal fin has a sapphire blue edging and the other fins carry white tips. The vertical body stripes range from black-and-white to black-and-yellow, depending on the native habitat location.

WHAT size?
Males 4cm, females 3cm.

WHAT does it eat?
Brineshrimp, daphnia, cyclops and small amounts of grindalworm; freeze-dried foods; micro-flake (not to be confused with fry food).

WHERE is it from?
Forest wetlands and savanna areas of West Africa.

WHAT does it cost?
★★☆☆☆
An inexpensive addition to the smaller community aquarium.

HOW do I sex it?
Males have more colour and longer fins. The females are fuller in the body and have clear fins.

WHAT kind of tank?
A community tank with other small fish, such as the sparkling gourami *(Trichopsis pumilis)*, dwarf spotted rasbora *(Rasbora maculata)*, Surinam blue stripe rivulus *(Rivulus xiphidus)*, dwarf corydoras such as *Corydoras pumilis* and other fish that share the same water conditions and do not grow any bigger than 4cm. In a species tank, several pairs can live together peacefully.

WHAT minimum size tank?
Species tank: 25x20x20cm. Community tank: size depends on the size, type and number of fish kept with the rocket panchax, but larger than a species tank.

WHAT kind of water?
Tolerates soft, dechlorinated tapwater, pH 6.5-7. Benefits from frequent water changes.

HOW warm?
21-25.5°C.

WHAT decor?
A well-planted tank containing Java moss, Java fern and *Anubias* spp., with floating plants such as Indian fern *(Ceratopteris thalictroides)*. The base of the tank can be kept clear or covered with fine sand.

WHAT area of the tank?
A surface-swimmer.

HOW many in one tank?
Large groups of equal numbers of males and females or a maximum of three pairs in a species tank.

HOW does it behave?
An active surface-swimmer, peaceful but good at jumping, so a tight-fitting aquarium lid is essential.

WILL it breed in an aquarium?
Yes, will spawn in a wool mop or fine-leaved plant such as Java moss. If the fish are kept in a species tank, the eggs and fry can be left with their parents, who will not eat them. The larger fry of the first generation will eat the smaller fry, as well as the smaller fry from subsequent generations, thus ensuring the survival of the fittest. Alternatively, remove fry from the tank (they will gather at the waterline) and raise them separately. They feed on infusoria and are slow to grow.

◀ *A little male rocket with a fiery tail, adding a touch of colourful activity in the upper half of the aquarium.*

Fundulopanchax gardneri
Gardner's killifish

FISH PROFILE

This killifish, formerly known as *Aphyosemion gardneri*, is found in many locations across Africa and has developed many different characteristics and a diversity of colour patterns. Variations in colour range from reds to bright blues and greens, which make these eye-catching fish a colourful addition to the hobby.

▲ *A colourful male F. gardneri nigerianum.*

WHAT size?
Males 7cm, females 6cm.

WHAT does it eat?
Flake and granular food; whiteworm; live, frozen and freeze-dried bloodworm and daphnia.

WHERE is it from?
West Africa: waters of the savannas and forests of western Cameroon and Nigeria.

WHAT does it cost?
★★★☆☆
Expect to pay varying prices for a pair, depending on the colour variation and the location habitat of these beautiful fish.

HOW do I sex it?
Males are larger, with much more vivid colours, and have extensions to the caudal fin. Females tend to have less vibrant colours on a brown background.

WHAT kind of tank?
Does best in a species tank, but will live in a well-planted community tank, where it adds a welcome splash of colour.

WHAT minimum size tank?
Species tank (for breeding): 30x20x20cm for one pair. Community tank: 60x30x30cm.

WHAT kind of water?
Slightly acidic, ph6.5, soft to medium-hard.

HOW warm?
22-26°C.

WHAT decor?
Species tank: Java moss and spawning mops. Peat substrate rather than a bare floor, if preferred. Community tank: Well-planted, including floating plants.

WHAT area of the tank?
Middle to top levels.

HOW many in one tank?
Several pairs can live together in a community aquarium or a larger, species-only tank.

HOW does it behave?
A relatively peaceful fish that settles well in a community aquarium.

WILL it breed in an aquarium?
Yes. To increase the chances of success, breed fish in a species aquarium. Place two or more pairs in a tank containing several spawning mops and Java moss. Fertilised eggs soon develop a black spot; non-fertilised ones turn white. Eggs hatch after 10-12 days and the fry can be left with the parents, where only the stronger ones survive. If fry are raised away from the parents, use water from the parental tank, which contains infusoria, the essential natural first food for fry. Be sure to prevent possible overfeeding and pollution caused by adding cultured infusoria. As fry emerge and grow at different rates and times, supplement feeding with newly hatched brineshrimp and microworms.

Fundulopanchax sjoestedti

Blue gularis

This fish used to be called *Aphyosemion sjoestedti* and has been in the aquarium hobby for many years. It is a large, superbly coloured fish with long, flowing, fringelike fins. The deep red-mauve body is overlaid with blue, orange and gold.

WHAT size?
Males 12.5cm, females 9cm.

WHAT does it eat?
Bloodworm, daphnia, glassworm, whiteworm, earthworms, mosquito larvae, granules and flake food.

WHERE is it from?
West Africa: southern Nigeria, western Cameroon and Ghana.

WHAT does it cost?
★★★☆☆   ★★★★☆
Large individuals usually command a higher price.

HOW do I sex it?
Males are considerably larger, with more vivid coloration. Females are almost brown in colour.

WHAT kind of tank?
Community or species tank.

WHAT minimum size tank?
Species tank: 45x30x30cm. Community tank housing other large fish: 90x30x38cm.

WHAT kind of water?
Best kept in soft to medium-hard water, at pH6-7.

HOW warm?
22-28°C.

WHAT decor?
A well-planted tank, with plenty of hiding places and floating plants for cover.

WHAT area of the tank?
A surface-feeder that likes to display in the middle of the tank.

HOW many in one tank?
In a community tank, one male is enough to be the centre of attraction, but he will live with as many females as you wish. In a species tank, one male to one female is best.

HOW does it behave?
Very active and impressive with, some people say, a tendency to be aggressive towards others of the same species. In a community aquarium it is best kept with larger tankmates, as it may eat small fish such as neons and guppies. Do not keep it with fish that will nip at its delicate, flowing fins.

WILL it breed in an aquarium?
Yes, however, this isn't easy and is best left to the more experienced aquarist. As with most peat-spawners, the resulting eggs need to be stored in the peat they were laid in and maintained at a constant temperature. The peat must neither be allowed to dry out nor be too wet, as this encourages the eggs to fungus. The procedure for hatching the eggs is the same as for *Australobias and Nothobranchius* spp. (see pages 123 and 128).

◄ *A strikingly beautiful, large male fish, dignified and impressive in any setting. These fish can be expensive because of their occasional limited availability and difficulty of aquarium breeding.*

Jordanella floridae

American flagfish

FISH PROFILE

▶ *Resilient yet beautiful, this little fish (male here) is a great introduction to killies for beginners.*

As its common name suggests, this fish displays the entire star-spangled splendour and colour of the American flag. It is a stocky little killie that tolerates all types of water ranges and temperatures, and is generally well tolerated in a community aquarium, making it an ideal fish for a beginner to keep.

WHAT size?
Males 6.5cm, females 5.5cm.

WHAT does it eat?
Vegetable-based flake foods, daphnia and freeze-dried and frozen bloodworm. Also tolerates algae wafers. Freely nibbles at live algae and plants.

WHERE is it from?
Florida, USA, where it is found in marsh areas, rivers, ditches and in some brackish locations.

WHAT does it cost?
★★☆☆☆
Reasonably cheap and within the reach of most pockets.

HOW do I sex it?
The very colourful males are green-blue, with red horizontal stripes running across the whole body. Each individual scale has subtle white edges, giving the fish its spangled appearance. A black spot – less visible than in the female of the species – can be seen in the middle of the body. The yellow-green females are dull by comparison, with a darker black spot in the middle of the body and a black spot behind the dorsal fin.

WHAT kind of tank?
Prospers in a well-planted community tank.

WHAT minimum size tank?
50x30x30cm.

WHAT kind of water?
Normal tapwater, pH7.5. Tolerates most ranges of water hardness. Some fish live naturally in slightly brackish water.

HOW warm?
Does better in cooler conditions, around 18°C, but will tolerate temperatures up to 28°C.

WHAT decor?
A well-planted tank with a wide range of live or plastic plants, or a combination of both, and plenty of hiding places.

WHAT area of the tank?
All levels, from the bottom of the tank to the top.

HOW many in one tank?
These fish will live quite happily in groups of six or more, but spawning pairs become protective (see below).

HOW does it behave?
Usually well tolerated in a community tank if kept with fish of a similar size or larger. However, when a male and female pair, they become protective of the spawning area and their behaviour towards other fish may change.

WILL it breed in an aquarium?
Yes, usually encouraged by a rise in temperature to around 25°C or higher. The fish deposit their eggs in areas of dense vegetation or in shallow pits dug in the gravel. The male guards the eggs and subsequent fry, and will aggressively drive away the female and other fish that may threaten his offspring.

Nothobranchius rachovii

Rachow's nothobranchius

FISH PROFILE

This is an extremely colourful, blood orange-and-blue fish, with a touch of black in the extreme edge of its caudal fin. The blue scales stand out against the orange background, creating a lace effect over the entire body. Just as striking is a magnificent black variety from Mozambique. *N. rachovii* is called an annual fish because it hatches, matures, spawns and dies all in less than a year. In the wild, it deposits eggs in the ground, where they remain until the following year's rainfalls. A few will hatch when the first rains arrive; the remainder hatch with the second and subsequent rainfalls, thus giving the species a greater chance of survival. Aquarium fish can be expected to follow a similar pattern.

WHAT size?
Males 5.5cm, females 4.5cm.

WHAT does it eat?
Tubifex, bloodworm, daphnia, glassworm, whiteworm, frozen foods and possibly flake food.

WHERE is it from?
Africa: from Mozambique south to the borders of South Africa.

WHAT does it cost?
★★★★☆
Expect to pay a little more. for a pair of fish.

HOW do I sex it?
Males are slightly larger and extremely colourful; females are brown, with a silver belly.

WHAT kind of tank?
Species or community tank.

WHAT minimum size tank?
Species tank: 30x25x20cm.
Community tank: 60x30x30cm.

WHAT kind of water?
Does well in soft water, at pH6-7. Will benefit from frequent water changes if kept in a small tank.

HOW warm?
20-24°C.

WHAT decor?
Species tank: peat fibre (for spawning) on the floor of a lightly planted tank, with space for free swimming. Community tank: spacious and well-planted, though not so densely as to reduce swimming space.

▼ *This male fish will add a vivid point of interest to the dullest aquarium.*

WHAT area of the tank?
Midwater to bottom.

HOW many in one tank?
Species tank: one male to several females. Community tank: several males will live together and add a splash of colour to the aquarium.

HOW does it behave?
With the clock ticking on this fish's relatively short life, males will compete vigorously with each other for the right to mate and will pester a female into submission. When females are introduced into a community aquarium, the strong spawning instinct can lead fish to attempt to spawn in gravel and they may sustain injury as a result. Good community tankmates include gouramis, barbs, rasboras, danios and corydoras catfish.

WILL it breed in an aquarium?
Yes. The most successful method is to set up a species tank with peat fibre on the base to a depth of 5cm and several hiding places for the females. The spawning embrace takes place in the peat fibre and the eggs are deposited there. Remove the peat with the eggs, squeeze out most of the water and place it in a plastic bag to 'rest'. This process simulates what would happen in nature. When you wish the eggs to hatch, place the peat in a tank with fresh, soft water and hatching will begin. Fry are easy to raise, and mature in about three months.

Rivulus xiphidus

Surinam blue-stripe rivulus

FISH PROFILE

A very small but colourful fish, with a purple-blue stripe running the length of the body against a background of orange-brown. The anal, pelvic and caudal fins have an orange-and-iridescent blue stripe. This shy and peaceful little killie will live in a community aquarium with other small (up to 2.5cm) delicate fish.

▲ *The male blue-stripe rivulus is beautiful, small and perfectly formed.*

WHAT size?
Males 4cm, females 3.5cm.

WHAT does it eat?
Brineshrimp, daphnia, cyclops, small bloodworm and glassworm.

WHERE is it from?
Northern South America: Surinam and French Guiana.

WHAT does it cost?
★★★☆☆ ★★★★☆
A pair of these beautiful fish is worth the relatively high price.

HOW do I sex it?
Males have more vibrant colours. Females are smaller and duller.

WHAT kind of tank?
Species tank or community aquarium with other small, delicate fish.

WHAT minimum size tank?
Species and community tanks: 25x20x20cm for several pairs.

WHAT kind of water?
Best kept in soft water, with a pH of 6-7. Benefits from frequent water changes.

HOW warm?
22-26°C.

WHAT decor?
A densely planted tank suits these shy fish. Java moss is ideal for this purpose.

WHAT area of the tank?
Bottom to middle areas of the tank, hiding amongst the vegetation.

HOW many in one tank?
Several pairs.

HOW does it behave?
Shy and peaceful, but like all *Rivulus* spp., it has a tendency to jump, so provide a tight-fitting lid.

WILL it breed in an aquarium?
Yes. For best results, keep a ratio of one male to two females in a species tank. Considering the small size of the fish, their eggs are quite large. Remove these from the Java moss and wool spawning mops in which they collect and place them in a small dish or tank away from the parents. Once hatched, feed the fry on infusoria at first. Before offering newly hatched brineshrimp, test that the fry are able to accept them by adding just a very small amount to the water. This is essential to avoid polluting the water with uneaten food. Fry that have eaten will have red stomachs, and further feeding with brineshrimp can then continue.

Beautiful air-breathers

▶ The anabantoids are probably the most diverse and varied of all freshwater fishes. The group contains the bubblenesting bettas and gouramis from Southeast Asia that are familiar to many hobbyists, the mouthbrooding species from the same area and free-spawning species from Africa. They all posses an auxiliary breathing organ, in addition to their gills, called the labyrinth organ, which consists of a series of folded membranes located in the head between the gills. Anabantoids breathe atmospheric air that they take in at the water surface, which means they can live in oxygen-poor conditions where fishes relying on gill respiration alone would not survive. Denying them access to the water surface would cause them to drown! Many anabantoids can be integrated into community tanks, where their attractive colours and interesting behaviour will enhance any aquarium.

Price guide

★	75p - £1
★★	£1 – £1.50
★★★	£1.75 – £2.50
★★★★	£2.75 – £4
★★★★★	£5 +

The enigmatic and graceful *Betta splendens* has been an aquarium favourite for many years. In terms of their resplendent colours and finnage forms, tank-bred varieties barely resemble wild-caught fish, but the behaviour and courtship of this species remain among the most recognisable in the world of fishkeeping. Its reputation as a fish that actively engages in fights with its own kind – even attacking its own reflection – is the stuff of legend.

▶ *A male* Betta splendens *spreads his fins as a show of strength.*

WHAT size?
Males and females 6cm.

WHAT does it eat?
Flake and frozen food, daphnia, bloodworms, brineshrimp and mosquito larvae.

WHERE is it from?
Originally all areas of Thailand, but its natural range has been extended to other areas in Southeast Asia.

WHAT does it cost?
★★☆☆☆
Cheap: many are commercially bred in Southeast Asia and imported in large numbers.

Betta splendens

Siamese fighting fish

WHAT area of the tank?
Mainly near the water surface.

HOW many in one tank?
Pairs or one male to two females in multiples to suit the size of the aquarium. Given the male's intense antagonism towards other males of the same species, never keep more than one male in a community.

HOW does it behave?
Males are generally fairly docile unless they come across another male, when they will engage in active fighting. Given two or more females in the tank, a male will divide his attentions among them.

WILL it breed in an aquarium?
Yes. Constructs a bubblenest at the surface, anchored to the tank sides or under a polystyrene tile or cup. Males are very rough with females during courtship and spawning. The pair embrace under the nest and the male collects the eggs. He places them in the nest and guards them and the fry until they are ready to swim freely. Aquarium rearing can be a problem, given the number of males in a single spawning that all require separate containers.

HOW do I sex it?
The domesticated variety is very easy to sex. Males have the long and flowing finnage, while females have less pronounced fins and are plumper in the belly. Often there is a small eggspot, or papilla, on her underside.

WHAT kind of tank?
A community tank with small and peaceful tankmates. Avoid fish that are liable to nip the trailing fins of the male betta.

WHAT minimum size tank?
Pairs can be kept in a tank as small as 30x30x30cm.

▶ *Female bettas are smaller, less flamboyant, but still elegant fish. Note the dark eggspot on her underside.*

WHAT kind of water?
Not important with domesticated varieties as they have been acclimatised to tapwater, but avoid extremes.

HOW warm?
24-28°C.

WHAT decor?
Planted tanks with plenty of surface cover.

Colisa lalia

Dwarf gourami

FISH PROFILE

One of the most popular and attractive of all aquarium fishes, the dwarf gourami has been an aquarium mainstay for many years. Several colour forms are now available, enhancing the reds and blues in the natural coloration of wild-caught fish.

WHAT size?
Males 5.5cm, females 5cm.

WHAT does it eat?
A varied and straightforward diet that includes flake and frozen food, daphnia, bloodworm, brineshrimp and mosquito larvae.

WHERE is it from?
India: West Bengal and Assam.

WHAT does it cost?
★★★☆☆
Reasonably priced. Many are commercially bred and imported from all over Southeast Asia and India.

HOW do I sex it?
Easy to sex at first viewing. Males are slightly larger and much more colourful. Wild fish have a red-brown base colour with alternating iridescent blue-green bars and dots to the finnage. Females are smaller and stouter, basically silver in colour, with some faint yellow barring to the body.

WHAT kind of tank?
Community tank with smaller and peaceful tankmates.

▼ *A male cobalt blue gourami boldly marked with red. The upturned mouth is clearly visible.*

WHAT minimum size tank?
Pairs can be kept in a tank as small as 30x25x25cm.

WHAT kind of water?
Slightly acidic, but will adapt to most tapwaters given time.

HOW warm?
21-26°C.

WHAT decor?
Planted tanks. Plenty of floating plants will encourage them to breed, and also provide refuge near the water surface.

◀ *Females have more subtle body patterns and are slightly smaller than males.*

WHAT area of the tank?

All areas, but prefers the surface in and around floating plants.

HOW many in one tank?

Pairs, or one male to two females in multiples to suit the size of the aquarium. Too many males will tend to squabble, and subordinate males are often very unhappy in the confines of a small community.

HOW does it behave?

Males are generally peaceful, although some individuals can be disruptive, being either aggressive or sulky. Males mixed with females keep themselves occupied, but always be aware that they are at their most aggressive when in breeding condition.

WILL it breed in an aquarium?

Yes. Constructs a bubblenest that includes plant pieces. Often, whole plants will be uprooted and bound together with bubbles. At this time no other fishes will be tolerated within the nest

area – even the female – until it is complete. The spawning embrace takes place underneath the nest and the glass-clear eggs float up into it. Following the spawning, the male looks after the eggs and fry. Fry of this species are often problematic and have a high mortality rate.

The royal red variety brings an attractive rusty hue to the aquarium palette. This is a male, with a more pointed dorsal fin.

The female has a rounded dorsal and more muted colours.

Colisa chuna

Honey gourami

FISH PROFILE

An easy-to-keep and rewarding little gourami, ideal for the smaller community aquarium. Can be kept in small groups. A good species to start with when considering a breeding project.

WHAT size?
Males 4cm, females 4.5cm.

WHAT does it eat?
Flake, frozen food, daphnia, bloodworms, brineshrimp and mosquito larvae.

WHERE is it from?
Brahmaputra Basin, Assam, Bangladesh.

WHAT does it cost?
★☆☆☆☆
Cheap to buy; many are commercially bred abroad and imported.

▼ *Unusually, female honey gouramis are larger than the males. Their colours are less intense.*

▶ *A male honey gourami in normal coloration. The colours deepen and intensify when the fish is displaying and breeding.*

HOW do I sex it?
Males are smaller and more colourful, especially at spawning time, with a deep honey colour on most of the body, plus a dark blue-black head and belly. Females are light brown with a darker brown longitudinal stripe from behind the operculum to the root of the tail.

WHAT kind of tank?
Community tank with smaller and peaceful tankmates.

WHAT minimum size tank?
Pairs can be kept in a tank as small as 30x20x20cm.

WHAT kind of water?
Slightly acidic to slightly alkaline, but fish will adapt to most tapwaters given time.

HOW warm?
21-26°C.

WHAT decor?
A planted tank with floating plants is ideal.

WHAT area of the tank?
All areas, but prefer the surface in and around floating plants.

HOW many in one tank?
You can mix a number of males with females in one tank. This encourages the males to display to each other and the females, and to show their best colours.

HOW does it behave?
Peaceful for most of the time. Males might spar with each other and circle regularly around females. Otherwise, attractive and inoffensive tank inhabitants.

WILL it breed in an aquarium?
Yes. Probably the best and easiest of the small gouramis to breed. The male constructs a rather tatty nest at the water surface and dances head-upward in front of the female to entice her into spawning. The pair embrace under the nest and the eggs are laid and fertilised there. The male guards them until the fry hatch and are free swimming. The jet black fry are easy to recognise and straightforward to raise.

Helostoma temminkii

Kissing gourami

FISH PROFILE

A larger gourami species, whose protrusible fleshy lips give the impression of kissing. Generally, the pink form is the most widely available, although green and yellow forms are offered for sale from time to time. Bred as a food fish in Southeast Asia.

▲ *The protrusible lips contain small teeth to feed on algae.*

WHAT size?
Males and females up to 30cm. However, this is the maximum size and unlikely in the home aquarium, where a good-sized specimen would grow to about half this size.

WHAT does it eat?
A largely vegetarian diet, including vegetable-based flake food, peas and cucumber. Fish rasp at algae on tank decor.

WHERE is it from?
Thailand, Java, Sumatra, Borneo.

WHAT does it cost?
★★★☆☆
Moderately expensive unless you buy smaller fish to grow on.

HOW do I sex it?
Almost impossible when not in breeding condition, and then the female is distinguishable by her gravid (egg-carrying) appearance.

WHAT kind of tank?
Larger community aquarium, with equally sized fish.

WHAT minimum size tank?
60cm long for one 15cm individual or two smaller fish.

WHAT kind of water?
Not particularly fussy regarding water composition. Conditioned tapwater will usually suffice.

HOW warm?
21-26°C.

WHAT decor?
Planted tank with plenty of bogwood, pipes and sunken pots.

WHAT area of the tank?
All areas, though often seen at the bottom of the tank.

HOW many in one tank?
Two or three maximum with other fishes; juveniles could be kept in greater numbers.

HOW does it behave?
Interesting to see two fish approach each other with their lips fully extended and appearing to kiss. It is unclear whether this behaviour is associated with sexual identification or two fish sparring. Otherwise, this species spends most of its time feeding on small algae around the decor in the tank.

WILL it breed in an aquarium?
Very difficult. This is a free-spawning species that lays thousands of eggs. Impractical for most home aquariums, given the quantities of fry that would need the tiniest of foods to start with.

▼ *Outside the breeding period, it is impossible to sex kissing gouramis.*

Macropodus opercularis

Paradisefish

FISH PROFILE

An extremely hardy, robust and colourful anabantoid, reputedly the first-ever ornamental 'tropical' freshwater species kept as a pet in Europe. It can almost be kept as a coldwater species. Easy to maintain, its only drawback is its aggression towards its own and other species.

WHAT size?
Males 9cm, females 8cm.

WHAT does it eat?
Does very well on flake foods, as well as virtually any other prepared or live foods.

WHERE is it from?
China, Vietnam, Korea and Taiwan.

WHAT does it cost?
★★★☆☆
Moderately priced for fully grown adult fish; small juveniles are less costly.

HOW do I sex it?
Males are larger and more colourful, with extended rays to the unpaired fins. Females are generally smaller and lack the flowing pennants of the males.

WHAT kind of tank?
Community tank with same-sized and robust species of fishes.

WHAT minimum size tank?
Pairs can be kept in a tank no smaller than 60x30x30cm.

WHAT kind of water?
Adapts well to most water values and compositions, even the more extreme ones, although these are not recommended.

HOW warm?
16-24°C.

WHAT decor?
A planted tank with plenty of floating plants.

WHAT area of the tank?
Stays mainly in the upper regions of the tank.

HOW many in one tank?
Given the propensity for males to fight and even be aggressive toward the females, keep only one pair in any tank. Avoid mixing males together.

HOW does it behave?
An active species that patrols its own territory, warding off intruders by flaring its finnage and opening its operculum (gill cover).

WILL it breed in an aquarium?
Yes. Spawning and raising the fry are straightforward. The main problem is the potential for aggression among the pair and towards other fishes in the tank. The male constructs a large bubblenest at the water surface amongst the floating plants. At this time, no other fishes are tolerated in the vicinity of the nest site. The female can be treated very roughly by the male during the spawning phase and should be removed directly afterwards. Several hundred eggs are laid and the male guards them and the fry until they are free swimming.

◄ Macropodus opercularis *is one of the hardiest of all aquarium fishes.*

Osphronemus goramy
Giant gourami

FISH PROFILE

The giant gourami – the largest of the anabantoid family – has been widely bred commercially as a food fish. The attractive juveniles are often on sale, but soon outgrow any small aquarium. Larger fish need specialist care if they are to thrive.

▲ *Do not be fooled into buying an attractive young giant gourami.*

WHAT size?
Males and females 60cm.

WHAT does it eat?
Their local name in some areas is 'water pig', so virtually anything, and lots of it.

WHERE is it from?
Originally thought to be from Java and Sumatra, but now found and bred all over Southeast Asia.

WHAT does it cost?
★★☆☆☆ ★★★★★
Tragically, juveniles are relatively cheap. However, adult and sub-adult specimens are fairly expensive.

▲ *The giant gourami is suitable only for the specialist or a public aquarium.*

HOW do I sex it?
The male's dorsal fin runs out to a point, and its forehead is rounded. In the female, the dorsal and anal fins are rounded.

WHAT kind of tank?
Only suitable for a very large tank or a public aquarium. Not feasible for most home set-ups.

WHAT minimum size tank?
At least 180x60x60cm for one specimen.

WHAT kind of water?
Adapts quite well to tapwater, given the quantities required.

HOW warm?
24°C.

WHAT decor?
Plants are impractical as they will be eaten or destroyed. Robust items of decor, such as rocks or large pieces of bogwood, are really the only option.

WHAT area of the tank?
All areas.

HOW many in one tank?
Keep singly.

HOW does it behave?
Normally very serene, and can be trained to take food from its owner's hand. Can become very skittish if frightened, and given its size this can be disastrous.

WILL it breed in an aquarium?
The simple answer is no, given the size of a mature pair, the potential for two to three thousand young and the space needed to raise them. In Southeast Asia, they are bred in large ponds and pools. The male constructs an almost spherical nest out of reeds and vegetation. Apparently, spawning takes place outside the nest and the eggs are carried into it. The eggs take 40 hours to hatch and the male guards the fry for a further 14 days.

Sphaerichthys osphromenoides

Chocolate gourami

FISH PROFILE

▶ *The fascinating chocolate gourami presents a challenge for the more experienced fishkeeper.*

The enigmatic chocolate gourami is a delicate fish from Southeast Asia that has enthralled anabantoid specialists for a long time. Originally thought to be a livebearer, it is in fact one of the few mouthbrooding gouramis, but its spawning behaviour was a mystery for many years. A challenging species of small gourami to keep and potentially to breed.

WHAT size?
Males and female 5.5cm.

WHAT does it eat?
Can be a fussy eater, taking mainly live foods that will fit into its rather small mouth. Mosquito larvae are a favourite, as are most live foods. Can be persuaded to take prepared food, but does best on live food.

WHERE is it from?
Southern part of the Malay Peninsula, Sumatra and Kalimantan (southern Borneo).

WHAT does it cost?
★★★☆☆
Despite being a difficult fish to keep, even a mature adult is surprisingly cheap to buy.

HOW do I sex it?
Very difficult outside the breeding period. Males and females can be distinguished from above, with the females looking slightly plumper. The finnage may offer some clues, but as this remains folded for long periods of time, this is also difficult.

WHAT kind of tank?
Small groups can be kept in a small, well-planted and dimly lit species aquarium or with small, acid water-loving species.

WHAT minimum size tank?
Up to ten fishes can be kept in a tank measuring 45x25x25cm.

WHAT kind of water?
Very fussy about water conditions. Strongly favours water that is clean, well-filtered, soft and acidic (pH4.8-6.5).

HOW warm?
21-28°C.

WHAT decor?
Heavily planted tanks are recommended, but given the acidity of the water, only plants such as Java moss (*Vesicularia dubyana*) and Java fern (*Microsorium pteropus*) will thrive in such an environment.

WHAT area of the tank?
All areas.

HOW many in one tank?
Several fish in one tank is acceptable, since aggression is not a problem.

HOW does it behave?
Can be shy and secretive, but once it has gained confidence in its surroundings and tankmates, it can be very active.

WILL it breed in an aquarium?
Yes, but the difficulty with setting up a tank for a specific breeding project is that the fish are hard to sex. They tend to choose a mate from a group and then exclude other fish from the spawning area. Sometimes fish will react to a change in temperature or an influx of cool water. A pair will form from the group of fishes and select a spawning site, usually a flat surface at the base of the tank. The spawning embraces take place here and the yellowish eggs are collected by the female (this species is a matriarchal carer). She mouthbroods the eggs for between 14 and 21 days before releasing the young. The fry do not return to the parent fish's mouth, as is seen in some cichlid species.

Trichogaster leeri
Pearl gourami

FISH PROFILE

One of the most instantly recognisable gourami species, the pearl gourami has been an aquarium favourite for many years and a mainstay of community tanks. The male's unpaired finnage can extend beyond the body and is covered in iridescent mother-of-pearl dots. A fairly long-lived species that will enhance virtually any community tank.

WHAT size?
Males and females 12cm.

WHAT does it eat?
All types of prepared food, from flake to frozen, as well as most small live foods.

WHERE is it from?
Malay Peninsula, Sumatra and Borneo.

WHAT does it cost?
★★★★☆
Juveniles are cheap, mature adults are moderately expensive.

HOW do I sex it?
Sexing these fishes becomes easier as they grow. Males have a pointed dorsal fin, whereas the female's is rounded. Males have longer and more flowing extensions to the unpaired fins and an orange chest, both of which are lacking in the females.

WHAT kind of tank?
Well-planted, moderately to brightly lit, with not too much surface movement.

WHAT minimum size tank?
Medium-sized, given the fish's potential growth. Keep pairs in a tank measuring at least 45x30x30cm.

WHAT kind of water?
Not at all fussy, although mainly found in slightly acidic, soft water. Conditioned tapwater will be fine once the fish have become acclimatised.

HOW warm?
21-28°C.

WHAT decor?
A heavily planted tank with plenty of floating plant material is ideal.

WHAT area of the tank?
All areas, but favours the upper level.

HOW many in one tank?
Integrating males and females is not a problem, in particular with young fish. Pairs or trios (one male to two females) are the best ratios.

HOW does it behave?
Does have the potential for being skittish when frightened. Otherwise, a very quiet and inoffensive fish.

WILL it breed in an aquarium?
Yes. Surface bubblenester, with the male constructing a nest within floating plant material. At this time, he will be aggressive towards other fishes in the area. The female joins him under the nest and the embrace produces floating, glass-clear eggs that are distributed amongst the bubbles. At the conclusion of the spawning, the female is driven away and the male tends to the nest. It has been observed that a male will construct a bubblenest, without a female present, and spit grains of sand into it. The reason for this interesting behaviour is unsure. Up to 2000 eggs are produced per spawning.

◀ The magnificent male boasts long, flowing finnage and shimmering coloration.

Ideal community fish

▶ Danios and rasboras originate from India and Southeast Asia and are closely related. They are generally peaceful and have an active, shoaling nature, although some can be quite timid. In their natural habitats they often experience seasonal changes in water conditions, making them ideally suited to a wide variety of aquarium water conditions. Some come from higher-altitude, moving waters and require well-filtered, oxygenated water; others that originate from low-lying swamps, ditches and rice fields are less demanding. Open swimming spaces are important, plus planted areas for cover and retreat. Most danios and rasboras are excellent community fish and good 'starter' choices for new aquariums or new fishkeepers. The majority are relatively small, although some species can grow to reasonable sizes, so make sure your aquarium is large enough to accommodate them when fully grown.

Price guide

★	60p – £1.20
★★	75p – £1.50
★★★	£1.00 – £1.75
★★★★	£1.25 – £2.50
★★★★★	£1.75 – £2.50

FISH PROFILE

As the common name suggests, this is one of the largest danios commonly available in the hobby. Giant danios sport an attractive and unusual patterning on the body, which makes them stand out from other aquarium fish. When buying them, check that the mouth shape is intact, as young fish can be easily spooked and often knock themselves on the glass, damaging the mouth. These fish are hardy and adaptable and make excellent tankmates for a lively aquarium of similar-sized fish.

WHAT size?
Males and females 12cm.

WHAT does it eat?
Dried pellets and flakes, as well as frozen foods, such as bloodworm, daphnia and brineshrimp.

WHERE is it from?
Asia; standing and moving waters, usually clear and well-oxygenated, with shaded areas and gravel bottoms.

WHAT does it cost?
★★★★☆
Relatively expensive, but to aquarists who appreciate these fish they represent good value for money.

Danio aequipinnatus

Giant danio

HOW do I sex it?
Males are thinner, with more defined patterns.

WHAT kind of tank?
Community with other peaceful and robust medium-sized fish.

WHAT minimum size tank?
90x30x30cm.

WHAT kind of water?
Undemanding, but prefers clear water with some movement.

HOW warm?
22-26°C.

WHAT decor?
Provide open swimming space, along with hiding spots amongst rocks and wood, plus a few planted areas.

WHAT area of the tank?
All levels.

HOW many in one tank?
Best kept in groups of at least four.

HOW does it behave?
Peaceful, active and lively. Because of its constant movement, delicate tankmates are not recommended.

WILL it breed in an aquarium?
Yes, breeds easily in good conditions, but the eggs and/or young are usually eaten in a community aquarium.

◀ *Body patterns vary with each fish and appear different under changing light conditions.*

▼ *The bony mouths of these fish are ideally suited to snatching food from the surface.*

Danio albolineatus

Pearl danio

FISH PROFILE

The pearl danio is so-called because of its smooth and iridescent body colour, which can vary between individuals. These fish are peaceful, active and undemanding, and will live happily with other peaceful fish. They appreciate areas of water movement and good aeration, as they swim rapidly and use up plenty of oxygen. Swimming space is important and whilst a long tank is required, it does not need to be deep or wide.

WHAT size?
Males 5cm, females 6cm.

WHAT does it eat?
Flake or dried foods, supplemented with small live or frozen foods.

WHERE is it from?
Clear, oxygen-rich flowing streams and rivers in Southeast Asia.

WHAT does it cost?
★★☆☆☆
Relatively inexpensive, hardy and easy to find in aquatic outlets.

▶ *Shoaling is an important part of these fishes' behaviour and they must be kept in groups.*

◀ *The golden form.*

HOW do I sex it?
Males are smaller, slender and more brightly coloured than females.

WHAT kind of tank?
Community with other small, active fish.

WHAT minimum size tank?
75x30x30cm.

WHAT kind of water?
Adapts easily to a wide range of pH and hardness conditions, but prefers well-filtered, flowing and oxygenated water.

HOW warm?
20-26°C.

WHAT decor?
Appreciates plenty of swimming space, along with some planted areas or hiding places around the back and sides of the aquarium.

WHAT area of the tank?
All levels.

HOW many in one tank?
Keep at least five together.

HOW does it behave?
Peaceful, active and constantly on the move. When the fish are in good condition there will be occasional squabbles between males, but this is normal.

WILL it breed in an aquarium?
Yes, relatively easily, but being an egg-scatterer, the eggs or newly hatched young are normally eaten. Fry can be raised by transferring pairs to a breeding tank and removing them after spawning.

Danio rerio

Zebra danio

FISH PROFILE

> Danios are constantly active and interact with each other, creating a lively community.

A popular aquarium fish of long-standing and often recommended as a first fish due to its hardy, peaceful and confident nature. A group will add a great deal of movement to the aquarium and liven up any display. A few colour morphs are available, including the equally popular leopard danio, often described as *Danio 'frankei'*, although whether it is a separate species or simply a variation is not clear. Both zebra and leopard danios are ideal for a small community environment.

WHAT size?
Males 6cm, females 6.5cm.

WHAT does it eat?
A micro-predator in the wild. Offer it some small frozen or live foods, such as daphnia, cyclops and small brineshrimp, as well as dried foods.

WHERE is it from?
Eastern India. Unlike some danios, this fish is often found in slow-moving and still waters, including streams, ditches and rice fields.

WHAT does it cost?
★★☆☆☆
These fish are captive-bred in huge numbers and remain very well priced.

HOW do I sex it?
Females are slightly larger and more rounded than males.

WHAT kind of tank?
Community aquarium.

WHAT minimum size tank?
60x30x30cm.

WHAT kind of water?
Undemanding of water conditions.

HOW warm?
18-24°C. Often prefers cooler water and can be kept in an unheated indoor aquarium.

WHAT decor?
Open swimming space plus densely planted areas.

WHAT area of the tank?
All levels.

HOW many in one tank?
A group of at least four.

HOW does it behave?
Peaceful and constantly active – an excellent community fish.

WILL it breed in an aquarium?
Yes, relatively easily. Spawning occurs in the morning amongst vegetation. The fish are egg-scatterers and a separate spawning and raising tank is normally required to prevent the eggs and young being eaten.

145

Rasbora trilineata

Scissortail rasbora

FISH PROFILE

Scissortails are robust and hardy and make excellent community fish for larger aquariums with similar-sized tankmates. Although not overly colourful, their 'scissor' markings are distinctive and add movement to the aquarium. The fish will adapt to, and live quite happily in, a variety of water conditions, but are at their best in slightly acidic, soft water. Because they are active and lively, delicate or timid tankmates are best avoided.

▲ *Although the scissortail's body is quite plain, the markings on the tail fin ensure that it stands out in the aquarium.*

WHAT size?
Males 14cm, females 13cm.

WHAT does it eat?
Flake, pellet and dried foods, supplemented with a variety of frozen or live foods.

WHERE is it from?
Open river and lake environments in Southeast Asia.

WHAT does it cost?
★★★☆☆
Considering its relatively plain coloration, the scissortail is a little more expensive than other fish in the group. Prices may vary depending on size.

HOW do I sex it?
Difficult to sex, but males are a little smaller and more slender than females.

WHAT kind of tank?
Community with other similar-sized fish.

WHAT minimum size tank?
90x30x30cm.

WHAT kind of water?
Adapts to a wide range of water conditions, including harder water. Natural water conditions are soft and acidic.

HOW warm?
24-26°C.

WHAT decor?
Provide plenty of swimming space, along with hiding places and vegetation around the edges.

WHAT area of the tank?
Mainly middle, but will inhabit all areas.

HOW many in one tank?
Best kept in groups of four or more.

HOW does it behave?
Peaceful and active.

WILL it breed in an aquarium?
Can be difficult to breed. Requires soft, acidic water, plus darker substrates and planted areas.

Tanichthys albonubes

White Cloud Mountain minnow

FISH PROFILE

An excellent aquarium fish that will do well under most conditions, although it does appreciate cooler water. Because of its size, it is best kept with other small tankmates in a community aquarium. White Clouds are active, hardy and undemanding. Long-finned and albino varieties are also offered for sale, and in recent years a few closely related species have also become available.

WHAT size?
Males and females 4cm.

WHAT does it eat?
Flake, small dried, frozen and live foods.

WHERE is it from?
Originates from the streams and moving waters of the White Cloud Mountain bordering China and Vietnam.

WHAT does it cost?
★☆☆☆☆
Very cheap and excellent value.

HOW do I sex it?
Males are thinner and more brightly coloured, while females are more rounded.

WHAT kind of tank?
Community with other small fish.

WHAT minimum size tank?
45x30x30cm.

WHAT kind of water?
Natural water conditions vary a great deal and the fish can be kept in a wide range of aquarium conditions.

HOW warm?
14-24°C. Prefers cooler water, and the fish can be kept in an unheated aquarium.

WHAT decor?
Appreciates a little surface cover, as well as a few hiding spots and open swimming spaces.

WHAT area of the tank?
All levels.

HOW many in one tank?
A group of at least four.

HOW does it behave?
Peaceful, shoaling and active.

WILL it breed in an aquarium?
Yes, relatively easily but the eggs and young are normally eaten in a community aquarium. To breed and raise fry successfully, place pairs of adults in a separate spawning tank.

▲ *White Clouds are an excellent addition to virtually any community of small fishes.*

Shimmering colours

▶ With their bright colours and peaceful disposition, rainbowfishes make ideal aquarium subjects, and many are easy to breed. They come from Australia and New Guinea and are adaptable to a range of water conditions. They are active top and midwater swimmers that need areas of open swimming space in the aquarium. While many can be classed as good community fish, there are species whose tankmates must be chosen with care. In fact, the best strategy is to keep the more delicate species in single-species tanks.

Melanotaenia is the largest and best-known genus amongst fishkeepers. The so-called 'blue eyes' belong to another increasingly popular group, which includes the forktail (*Pseudomugil furcatus*). Rainbowfishes breed in a similar manner to killifishes. After a brief courtship, the female deposits a single egg onto fine-leaved plants or spawning mops.

Price guide

★	Up to £1
★★	£2
★★★	£3
★★★★	£4
★★★★★	£5

An attractive fish, well suited to the smaller aquarium. Although it has a reputation for being delicate, it is quite hardy if not subjected to sudden changes in temperature and water conditions. Acclimatise it gradually to the water in its new home.

WHAT size?
Males 5cm, females 3.5cm.

WHAT does it eat?
Dried foods and frozen bloodworm. Supplement the diet with live foods, such as daphnia and brineshrimp.

WHERE is it from?
Northern Australia and Irian Jaya (western New Guinea), Indonesia. The New Guinea fish are darker and carry more red colours than the Australian fish.

WHAT does it cost?
★★★☆☆
Moderately expensive.

▲ *A male fish of the yellow form from Australia. The fin extensions are used to display to potential mates.*

Iriatherina werneri

Threadfin rainbowfish

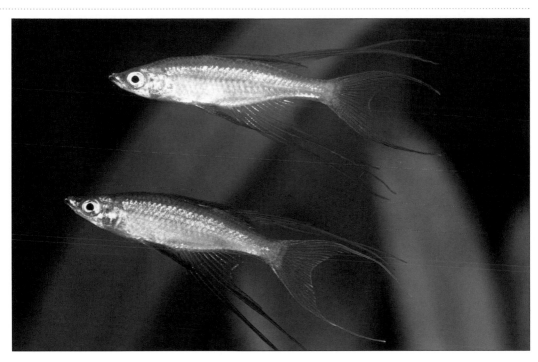

HOW do I sex it?
Males have long threadlike extensions on the dorsal and anal fins. Females lack these long fins and have less colour.

WHAT kind of tank?
A community tank with other peaceful fish, but best seen in a species tank.

WHAT minimum size tank?
45x20x20cm.

WHAT kind of water?
Good-quality, very soft to soft, slightly acidic to neutral (pH6-7).

HOW warm?
24-28°C.

WHAT decor?
In the wild, it is found in slow-moving streams with abundant vegetation. Provide a well-planted aquarium.

WHAT area of the tank?
Midwater.

HOW many in one tank?
Keep in groups of five or more.

▲ *Two males of the New Guinea red form. Rainbowfish colours appear to shimmer, hence their common name.*

HOW does it behave?
A peaceful fish. Males will display to each other by spreading their long fins, but will not cause injury.

WILL it breed in an aquarium?
Yes, placing tiny, sticky eggs on fine-leaved plants. If possible, remove the plants with the eggs attached to a separate tank to hatch. This takes 8-12 days.

Melanotaenia boesemani

Boeseman's rainbowfish

A popular and beautiful rainbowfish, but males do not attain their full colours until they are about 12 months old. Keep this very active shoaling fish in a tank with gentle water movement. Provide a well-fitting cover, as it is a good jumper.

WHAT size?
Males 10cm, females 8cm.

WHAT does it eat?
Flake and frozen foods. Offer live foods as well.

WHERE is it from?
The Ajamaru Lakes region of Irian Jaya (western New Guinea), Indonesia.

WHAT does it cost?
★★★★★
Relatively expensive. Star rating is for a 5cm young fish. Adult fish will cost more.

▲ *Young fish, just showing colour.*

▲ *One of the most popular rainbowfish because of its stunning colours. These take up to a year to develop.*

HOW do I sex it?
Males are larger and have a deeper body than the females. Females lack the bright orange colour of the males.

WHAT kind of tank?
Well suited to a community tank, but in a species tank a shoal of Boeseman's rainbowfishes is a stunning sight.

WHAT minimum size tank?
90x30x30cm.

WHAT kind of water?
Fairly soft, slightly acidic to alkaline (pH 6.6-8).

HOW warm?
25-30°C.

WHAT decor?
Planted tank with fine gravel or sand substrate.

WHAT area of the tank?
Top and midwater.

HOW many in one tank?
Keep at least one pair in a community tank. If housing a shoal in a single-species aquarium, be sure to observe the correct stocking levels for the tank size.

HOW does it behave?
A very active shoaling fish, but peaceful with other fish.

WILL it breed in an aquarium?
Yes. It spawns over fine-leaved plants such as Java moss. If kept with other fish in a community tank, the eggs may be eaten.

Melanotaenia praecox

Neon, or dwarf, rainbowfish

FISH PROFILE

A peaceful and very attractive aquarium fish – males have striking colours. The ideal rainbowfish for the smaller community aquarium.

WHAT size?
Males and females 5cm.

WHAT does it eat?
Flake foods, supplemented with frozen and live foods.

WHERE is it from?
Mameramo River in Northern Irian Jaya (western New Guinea), Indonesia.

WHAT does it cost?
★★★★☆ ★★★★★
Reasonably expensive.

HOW do I sex it?
Males are brightly coloured, with red fins and a blue sheen on the body. They are also deeper in the body than the female, which is silver with yellow-orange fins.

WHAT kind of tank?
Will do well in a community tank with fish its own size and the same temperament. Or just keep a shoal in a single-species tank.

WHAT minimum size tank?
60x25x25cm.

WHAT kind of water?
Medium-hard, neutral (pH7).

HOW warm?
23-28°C.

WHAT decor?
Planted tank with fine gravel or sand substrate.

WHAT area of the tank?
Midwater.

HOW many in one tank?
Do not keep singly – have at least one pair. A group of five would make a good show of colour.

HOW does it behave?
A peaceful and active shoaling fish.

WILL it breed in an aquarium?
Yes. As with most rainbowfishes, it will breed in a community tank, but is best bred in a separate set-up.

▼ *A beautiful male* M. praecox. *This rainbowfish is a prolific spawner whose eggs hatch in 10-12 days.*

Melanotaenia trifasciata

Banded rainbowfish

FISH PROFILE

One of the larger rainbowfishes and an excellent addition to the community aquarium. A group will provide a dazzling display of colour. A good subject for a first attempt at breeding rainbowfish.

WHAT size?
Males 12cm, females slightly smaller.

WHAT does it eat?
Flake and frozen foods. An algae-based formula prevents them eating soft plants. Additional live foods are a bonus.

WHERE is it from?
Australia: Northern Territory and Queensland.

WHAT does it cost?
★★★★★
Relatively expensive.

HOW do I sex it?
Males are larger, with a deeper body shape and more intense coloration. Also, the rays on the front dorsal fin and anal fin of males are pointed.

WHAT kind of tank?
Community tank or a rainbowfish species-only tank.

WHAT minimum size tank?
90x30x30cm.

WHAT kind of water?
Medium-hard, slightly acidic to alkaline (pH6.6-8).

HOW warm?
24-28°C.

WHAT decor?
A well-planted tank.

WHAT area of the tank?
Top and midwater.

HOW many in one tank?
Best kept in a group. A ratio of three males to two females is ideal.

HOW does it behave?
A lively fish but not usually aggressive. It may eat soft-leaved plants.

WILL it breed in an aquarium?
Yes, this is one of the easiest rainbowfishes to breed. It deposits sticky eggs on fine-leaved plants. Remove the plants and eggs to a separate tank to hatch, which takes seven days. If left in the tank, other fish will eat the eggs. Can be a relatively prolific breeder.

▼ *M. trifasciata can be found with red or yellow fins. Although* Melanotaenia *females are less vivid, keeping both sexes together encourages males to show of their best.*

Pseudomugil furcatus
Forktail rainbowfish

FISH PROFILE

A beautiful fish, well suited to the smaller aquarium. It can be somewhat shy but loses this trait if given plenty of plant cover. Classed as one of the 'blue eyes' that inhabit fresh and brackish waters of Australia and New Guinea.

▶ *A male* Pseudomugil furcatus*, one of the group of rainbowfishes called 'blue eyes'. All the species in this group are rather small.*

WHAT size?
Males 5.5cm, females 4.5cm.

WHAT does it eat?
Good-quality flake foods, plus frozen foods, including bloodworm. Relishes small live foods, such as daphnia.

WHERE is it from?
Eastern New Guinea (Papua).

WHAT does it cost?
★★★★☆
Reasonably expensive.

HOW do I sex it?
The male is more brightly coloured and has a longer first dorsal fin than the rather plain female.

WHAT kind of tank?
Fine in a community tank with other small peaceful fish. It does well with other rainbowfishes, such as *Iriatherina werneri*. A shoal looks good in a species tank, which is often suggested as the best way to keep it.

WHAT minimum size tank?
45x20x20cm.

WHAT kind of water?
Not too soft and slightly alkaline (pH7.2-7.9).

HOW warm?
24-26°C.

WHAT decor?
Planted tank with a fine gravel or sand substrate.

WHAT area of the tank?
Midwater.

HOW many in one tank?
Do not keep singly. Looks best in a group of no fewer than five.

HOW does it behave?
Lively but peaceful shoaling fish.

WILL it breed in an aquarium?
Yes. While it will breed in a tank with other fish, the best method is to set up a separate tank with a clump of fine-leaved plants, such as Java moss. There the fish can deposit their sticky eggs, which will hatch in 15-20 days.

Lively and easy to breed

▶ Among the livebearing toothcarps you will find some of the most popular species in the fishkeeping hobby. Cultivated guppies, platies, mollies and swordtails are available in a huge diversity of colours and fin shapes. However, true breeding strains are difficult to maintain. Selective breeding is essential, as these cultivated fish will always revert to the wild form. After a gestation period, the female gives birth to fully formed young fishes. At birth, these tiny replicas of their parents only lack their colour and mature finnage. Fewer young are born compared with egglayers, but their chances of survival are much greater due to their size and mobility.

The goodeids, two of which are featured here, are very different. The young are fed internally, attached to the parent by feeding tubes. Since the gestation period is longer, the young are larger than those of most poeciliids.

Price guide

★	£3 – 4
★★	£5 – 6.50
★★★	£7 – 8.50
★★★★	£10
★★★★★	£20

FISH PROFILE

This robust-bodied species shows indifferent colour when young, but a fully mature male displays beautiful coloration that Dr Robert Rush Miller (the celebrated American ichthyologist) described as 'splendid' when he first saw it in the wild. Widely bred and distributed through the trade.

WHAT size?
Males 7.5cm, females 9cm.

WHAT does it eat?
All foods. It has an enormous appetite and thrives on a mix of live, flake and frozen foods.

WHERE is it from?
One region only, the Rio Ameca drainage, Mexico.

WHAT does it cost?
★★★☆☆
Reasonably inexpensive.

Ameca splendens

Butterfly goodeid

HOW do I sex it?
In the male, the first few rays of the anal fin are bunched together and shortened to produce a notch. Males also have an enlarged dorsal fin. Females are much drabber.

WHAT kind of tank?
Community tank with robust species of similar size, such as barbs. A colony tank with its own kind is another option.

WHAT minimum size tank?
75x30x30cm.

WHAT kind of water?
Clean and well-oxygenated, medium to medium-hard, neutral to slightly alkaline (pH7-7.4), but this is a very adaptable species.

HOW warm?
Appreciates cooler water at 20-24°C.

▼ *A mature male Ameca splendens, showing adult colour and finnage.*

▲ *An attractive, robust female. After an elaborate courtship, females produce one brood following a mating.*

WHAT decor?
Some plant cover, but plenty of open swimming spaces.

WHAT area of the tank?
All areas.

HOW many in one tank?
Only limited by the dimensions of the tank.

HOW does it behave?
Do not keep with delicate or slow-moving fishes. Its robust physique and pushy, hungry habits are no problem for like-minded fishes.

WILL it breed in an aquarium?
Yes, but fry may not survive in the community tank. Move the female to a heavily planted tank for best results.

Belonesox belizanus

Pike topminnow

FISH PROFILE

A large, beaky mouth equipped with sharp, needlelike teeth allows this predator to eat fish up to half its body length, including its own siblings. Large females may eat their own mates. The pike topminnow lurks in the vegetation, but only kills to eat and is quite a nervous species.

WHAT size?
Males 15cm, females 20cm.

WHAT does it eat?
This is a live food-only species, which means live fish. Newborns can possibly be weaned onto other food, but will not flourish.

WHERE is it from?
Atlantic coast of Mexico from Veracruz state southwards to Nicaragua.

WHAT does it cost?
★★★★☆
Moderately priced. Large adult specimens are more expensive but rarely available.

HOW do I sex it?
As the fish matures, the thickened rays of the anal fin fold over to form a rodlike structure called the gonopodium.

WHAT kind of tank?
Species tank – this is not a community fish.

WHAT minimum size tank?
90x30x30cm. A roomy aquarium is not necessary as the fish does not move around much, other than when it dashes out for food.

WHAT kind of water?
Adapts to most water conditions.

HOW warm?
24-28°C.

WHAT decor?
A planted tank with some floating plants.

WHAT area of the tank?
Upper level.

HOW many in one tank?
One pair only.

HOW does it behave?
Generally peaceful, apart from its eating habits.

WILL it breed in an aquarium?
Yes, breeds easily, but raising the fry is extremely difficult because of feeding problems. Large females can produce 200 fry, each needing one live baby fish per day. If not well fed they will eat each other, preying on the smallest.

▼ *Note the long gonopodium of this male pike topminnow. It is used to transfer sperm to the female and the eggs are fertilised inside the female.*

Dermogenys pusilla

Wrestling halfbeak

FISH PROFILE

An interesting, streamlined fish, with large, winglike pectoral fins. Males have aggressive tendencies towards each other but are otherwise peaceful. Newly imported specimens are often weak, succumbing easily to disease, so quarantining them is essential.

WHAT size?
Males 3.5cm, females 5cm.

WHAT does it eat?
These surface-feeders accept mosquito larvae, fruit flies and other live foods. They will take flake and frozen foods, but not from the bottom of the tank.

WHERE is it from?
Thailand, Malaysia, Java, Sumatra, Singapore and Indonesia.

WHAT does it cost?
★★★☆☆
Good-sized specimens are moderately expensive.

OTHER SPECIES
The orange-finned halfbeak (*D. ebrardtii*) from Sulawesi, Indonesia is also available in the hobby. The dorsal, anal and tail fins are bright orange, more so in males.

▲ *The wrestling halfbeak is one of the smaller* Dermogenys *species. As the common name suggests, the male can lock its beak with that of another male in wrestling combat.*

HOW do I sex it?
In males, the first few rays of the anal fin are shorter than the rest. In females, the first few rays are the same length or longer. The colours of the female are the same as those of the male, but paler.

WHAT kind of tank?
Community of similarly sized fish.

WHAT minimum size tank?
60x30x30cm.

WHAT kind of water?
Medium to medium-hard, neutral to slightly alkaline (pH7-7.4), with good filtration.

HOW warm?
23-26°C.

WHAT decor?
Some surface plant cover and open swimming areas.

WHAT area of the tank?
Surface-swimmer.

HOW many in one tank?
One pair or one male to several females. Males can be quarrelsome and fight.

HOW does it behave?
Hardy and peaceful. A skittish species that needs a tight tank cover.

WILL it breed in an aquarium?
Yes, but isolate the female, because although the fry are large at birth, they may be eaten in a community aquarium.

Heterandria formosa

Dwarf topminnow

This charming species, which can be kept in an unheated tank in a warm room, is very suitable for children, who can observe its interesting breeding habits. Due to its diminutive size, it is best kept with its own kind in a colony tank.

WHAT size?
Males 1.5-2cm, females 3cm.

WHAT does it eat?
Flake and frozen foods, but needs some live food, such as brineshrimp.

WHERE is it from?
Southern USA.

WHAT does it cost?
★☆☆☆☆
Inexpensive.

▲ *The female is twice the size of the male and carries fry at different stages of development inside her.*

▲ *The tiny male is a delightful fish. Due to their very small size, dwarf topminnows are best kept with their own kind.*

COLONY TANK

Some small livebearer species really need to be colony-bred. In this situation, three generations live together in harmony, and newborns are not molested by adults. The dwarf topminnow is a tiny fish that flourishes in a tank with its own kind. Newborns are immediately accepted into the colony.

HOW do I sex it?
As males mature, the anal fin changes shape and forms a rodlike gonopodium.

WHAT kind of tank?
Colony tank.

WHAT minimum size tank?
45x25x25cm.

WHAT kind of water?
Medium to medium-hard, neutral to slightly alkaline (pH7-7.4).

HOW warm?
20-24°C, but will tolerate higher temperatures.

WHAT decor?
A well-planted tank.

WHAT area of the tank?
Midwater to surface swimmer.

HOW many in one tank?
As many as the colony will sustain.

HOW does it behave?
An undemanding, peaceful species.

WILL it breed in an aquarium?
Yes, will colony breed. Brood numbers are small, and individuals can be born at intervals of several days. Provide *Riccia fluitans* at the surface for the fry to hide in.

Limia nigrofasciata

Humpbacked limia

FISH PROFILE

This peaceful species shows off its most splendid colours in an aquarium that receives some natural daylight. It appreciates some green algae in the tank. The high, humpy back, from which the species gets its common name, only develops in mature males.

WHAT size?
Males and females 8cm.

WHAT does it eat?
A good mix of foods, including some green vegetable matter and live food. Not a fussy eater.

WHERE is it from?
Haiti.

WHAT does it cost?
★★★☆☆
Moderately priced. Good-quality, mature specimens cost more.

▶ *In this beautifully marked pair of humpbacks, the male (top) displays his magnificent dorsal fin.*

FLOCK BREEDING
Flock breeding occurs where the females are not isolated to give birth. Given adequate cover, most newborns will survive in a species tank. Several generations can live together, forming a 'flock' that interbreeds.

HOW do I sex it?
Mature males have a rodlike extension formed by the anal fin rays (the gonopodium), a high, humpy back and a fleshy growth along the ventral surface between the gonopodium and caudal peduncle (the base of the tail fin). The dorsal fin is also much enlarged.

WHAT kind of tank?
Suitable for a community aquarium, but a single-species tank of 20 or more adults in a 90x30x30cm aquarium is very attractive.

WHAT minimum size tank?
60x30x30cm.

WHAT kind of water?
Medium to medium-hard, neutral to slightly alkaline (pH7-7.4).

HOW warm?
22-28°C. The fish prefer the upper part of this range.

WHAT decor?
A heavily planted tank provides good cover for harassed females.

WHAT area of the tank?
Midwater-swimmer.

HOW many in one tank?
One male to three females in a minimum size aquarium, as males are persistent chasers.

HOW does it behave?
A lively, peaceful species that is suitable for a community aquarium. Heavily pregnant females need refuges in which to hide from male harassment.

WILL it breed in an aquarium?
In a species-only tank with plenty of cover, this species will flock-breed. Some fish could survive in a heavily planted community aquarium, but it is doubtful.

Poecilia reticulata

Guppy

FISH PROFILE

A lively, colourful, peaceful community fish that is easy to keep and breed. The real challenge comes with selective breeding, fixing the strain to breed true to type. Specialised breeding has produced many tail varieties. Veiltails are produced in many colour forms available through the trade, but do not expect them to breed true to type.

WHAT size?
Males 3cm, females 5cm.

WHAT does it eat?
Flake and frozen foods, plus live foods such as brineshrimp.

WHERE is it from?
Originates from Venezuela and Caribbean islands, including Barbados, Trinidad and Antigua, but widely spread for mosquito control. Fancy varieties are farm bred.

WHAT does it cost?
★☆☆☆☆
Inexpensive, but line-bred pairs from a specialist breeder will cost more.

▶ *Although not highly coloured, these blonde guppies have a pleasing appearance, with red overlaying the basic gold body hue. The male has more intense colour than the female shown above it.*

HOW do I sex it?
As males mature, the rays of the anal fin thicken to form a rodlike structure called the gonopodium. The female's anal fin appears fanlike when spread.

WHAT kind of tank?
Community aquarium.

WHAT minimum size tank?
45x25x25cm.

WHAT kind of water?
Medium to medium-hard, neutral to slightly alkaline (pH7-7.4).

HOW warm?
20-26°C.

WHAT decor?
A well-planted tank that includes some floating plants to provide surface cover, plus open swimming areas.

WHAT area of the tank?
Midwater to surface level.

HOW many in one tank?
At least two pairs.

HOW does it behave?
A peaceful community fish, but do not keep long-finned guppy varieties with fin-nippers.

WILL it breed in an aquarium?
Yes, it's not called the millions fish for nothing! Some fry will survive in heavily planted tanks.

◀ Colour, pattern and tail-shape dictate the names of the many varieties available in the hobby today.

▼ The cobra, or snakeskin, pattern that covers the body is clear to see in this fish.

▶ The guppy has been developed in tail patterns and colours to suit all tastes, but do not expect them to breed true.

163

Poecilia velifera

Sailfin molly

FISH PROFILE

Wild specimens vary in size and quality, but at its best this is a spectacular fish when displaying its high, long-based dorsal fin. Wild fish are blue-green, but have been hybridised with *Poecilia latipinna* and other mollies to produce many colour varieties. The all-black, high-finned molly with an orange border to the dorsal fin is one handsome variety rarely available nowadays, but there are plenty more to choose from.

WHAT size?
Males 15cm, females 18cm.

WHAT does it eat?
Easily fed on flake and frozen foods. Live foods should form part of a well-balanced diet.

WHERE is it from?
Yucatan, Mexico.

WHAT does it cost?
★★★☆☆ ★★★★★
Good mature specimens can be expensive. Wild fish rarely available.

◀ *The jet-black sailfin molly is a striking fish with a high dorsal fin edged in orange.*

HOW do I sex it?
As the fish matures, the thickened rays of the anal fin fold over to form a rodlike structure called the gonopodium. The female's anal fin appears fanlike when spread. Females are larger, but both sexes display excellent colour.

WHAT kind of tank?
Community with robust fishes. They also live together happily in a colony.

WHAT minimum size tank?
90x30x45cm.

WHAT kind of water?
Good filtration and high-quality water are very important. Provide medium-hard to hard, neutral to slightly alkaline (pH7-7.4) water. Will also accept brackish conditions. In poor water conditions, fish may shimmy, meaning they swim in a slow, weaving motion from side to side.

HOW warm?
24-28°C – these fish will thrive in warm conditions.

▲ *The large dorsal fin of this colour variety can take a long time to reach its full potential.*

▼ Green sailfin molly. The male has the magnificent dorsal fin typical of the variety. The female's is much closer to the body and her colours are more muted.

WHAT decor?
A well-planted tank with plenty of open swimming space. Do not use bogwood or other items that acidify the water.

WHAT area of the tank?
Midwater, but will feed at the surface.

HOW many in one tank?
As many as appropriate for the size of the tank. Two females to one male if just keeping a trio.

HOW does it behave?
Being hardy and peaceful, it is a good community dweller. Displays well when happy.

WILL it breed in an aquarium?
Yes. Molly young often survive in community tanks, but the high-fin type will only reach their full potential in specially set up breeding and rearing conditions.

▼ This silver lyretail sailfin molly looks striking when seen against a dark background.

Poecilia sphenops

Black molly

FISH PROFILE

Many colour morphs occur in nature. In some populations, the body colour of the dominant male is black, and many wild mollies are black-speckled, with dark dorsal and caudal fins. However, the all-black mollies have been produced by selective breeding.

WHAT size?
Males 6.5cm, females 8cm.

WHAT does it eat?
Flake and frozen foods, worms. Vegetable matter is not essential. Mollies are hungry all the time and not fussy feeders, but really appreciate live food.

WHERE is it from?
Wide-ranging in Mexico and southwards to Colombia.

WHAT does it cost?
★★☆☆
Moderately priced.

HOW do I sex it?
As males mature, the rays of the anal fin thicken and fold over to form a rodlike structure called the gonopodium. The female's anal fin appears fanlike when spread.

WHAT kind of tank?
A roomy community tank.

WHAT minimum size tank?
60x30x30cm.

WHAT kind of water?
Medium to medium-hard and neutral to slightly alkaline (pH7-7.4), with some aeration. Soft water is not appreciated. Acclimatisation can be problematic due to fresh-salt-fresh water changes during transportation. *P. sphenops* does not originate in salty water – it is a freshwater fish – hence the problems.

HOW warm?
26-28°C. Although temperatures of 20°C have been recorded in the wild, mollies in the aquarium appreciate warm conditions.

WHAT decor?
Provide a well-planted tank. Do not use bogwood or any other acidifying material. Coral sand makes a good substrate.

WHAT area of the tank?
Middle to upper levels.

HOW many in one tank?
A couple of pairs.

HOW does it behave?
A robust, lively species that thrives when conditions are to its liking.

WILL it breed in an aquarium?
Yes, and some youngsters will survive in a heavily planted tank, as they are 8mm long at birth and grow rapidly in the right conditions.

▲ *A black, short-finned female. Note the upturned mouth, ideal for feeding at the water surface.*

◀ *Good-quality males of this variety should be a velvety black all over.*

Xenotoca eiseni

Redtailed goodeid

FISH PROFILE

The red caudal peduncle gives this very deep-bodied, chunky fish its common name. Aggressive tendencies are very apparent in those fish that have been reared on their own or not heavily fed. This fish has been available through the trade for many years.

◀ *The female is rather drab by comparison with the male fish.*

▲ *The red area on the caudal peduncle of the male gives this species its common name.*

WHAT size?
Males 6cm, females 7cm.

WHAT does it eat?
Greedily accepts flake, frozen and live foods. Several smaller feeds a day will keep it happy.

WHERE is it from?
Central Highlands of Mexico.

WHAT does it cost?
★★☆☆☆
Moderately priced.

HOW do I sex it?
Males are very brightly and attractively coloured, females are drab. Males have a notched anal fin.

WHAT kind of tank?
If reared with fish of the same robust disposition, aggression is greatly reduced, but this is not an ideal community fish.

WHAT minimum size tank?
60x30x30cm.

WHAT kind of water?
Well-filtered, medium to medium-hard, neutral to slightly alkaline (pH7-7.4).

HOW warm?
22-26°C.

WHAT decor?
A well-planted aquarium.

WHAT area of the tank?
All levels.

HOW many in one tank?
A couple of pairs if reared with other robust fish.

HOW does it behave?
If well fed and reared with tankmates, aggression (i.e. fin-nipping) is greatly reduced.

WILL it breed in an aquarium?
Yes, but few fry will survive in a community aquarium.

Xiphophorus maculatus
Southern platy

A deep-bodied species, with many colour forms found in nature. The perfect community fish, being peaceful and adaptable. Has been hybridised with swordtails to produce the myriad colours and fin forms seen in the trade. Pure stock is only available through specialist breeders.

▶ *The marigold platy has a basic colour of yellow, deepening to orange towards the rear, becoming blood-red at the base of the tail.*

◀ *The wagtail platy is a well-established strain, available in colours from pale yellow to deep red. Finnage and lips should be jet-black.*

WHAT size?
Males 4.5cm, females 5.5cm.

WHAT does it eat?
Flake and live foods.

WHERE is it from?
Originates in Mexico, Belize and Guatemala. Cultivated hybrids are farm-bred.

WHAT does it cost?
★★☆☆☆   ★★★☆☆
Moderately priced. Large mature line-bred fish at the upper end of this price rating.

▼ *Some black varieties have blue iridescent scales, which are quite attractive and do not detract from the beauty of the fish.*

HOW do I sex it?
Males have a long rodlike structure formed by the anal fin rays; the female's anal fin is fanlike.

WHAT kind of tank?
Community aquarium.

WHAT minimum size tank?
60x30x30cm.

WHAT kind of water?
Medium to medium-hard, neutral to slightly alkaline (pH7-7.4).

HOW warm?
22-26°C.

WHAT decor?
Well-planted, but do not use any items that acidify the water, such as bogwood.

WHAT area of the tank?
A midwater swimmer.

HOW many in one tank?
Keep a pair or two, as you like.

HOW does it behave?
A very good, peaceful community fish that tolerates a wide range of aquarium conditions and is not a fussy eater.

WILL it breed in an aquarium?
Yes, but the young will probably not survive in a community aquarium. Even the parents will consider the fry a meal.

VARIABLE PLATY
Xiphophorus variatus

This fish ranges through Central America, and a wide variety of colour forms occurs throughout. It is more slender than *X. maculatus*, but otherwise this peaceful, adaptable community fish has all the same requirements. It has been hybridised with *X. maculatus* (the southern platy) and *X. helleri* (the swordtail) to produce the many varieties bred in fish farms for the trade and sold as platies. Wild specimens are only available through specialists.

◀ *A male sunset hi-fin with intense colours.*

▼ *The female has a more subtle colour palette.*

▼ *This is an attractive mixed group of sunset varieties.*

Sleek and stylish

▶ Loaches are well known for their active, playful nature and unusual habits. In particular, some loaches 'rest' on their sides or in odd positions, but this is no cause for concern. Loaches have no scales, which gives them a sleek appearance, but also makes them more sensitive to chemicals and treatments, which are absorbed into the body far more quickly than in other fish. Since loaches are scavengers, be sure to provide a smooth substrate that will not damage their barbels. Hiding spots are important for them, as well as social interaction. Given a large tank with many retreats, some loach species will cram themselves together, hiding in the same place, while other individuals may select and defend their own spot. Within the 'sharks', some fish are closely related whilst others are not, but all share the sleek body shape and bold dorsal fin from which they get their common name.

Price guide

★	Up to £2
★★	£2 – 4
★★★	£4 – 6
★★★★	£6 – 8
★★★★★	£8 – 10

FISH PROFILE

Its attractive, sleek appearance, combined with its 'shark' name and peaceful nature, account for the silver shark's popularity amongst fishkeepers. Its only drawback is its fully grown size – up to 30cm – which makes it too large for most aquariums. Being a shoaling fish, it should be kept in a group of three, and three adults will need a 150cm aquarium. Apart from this, the fish are easy to care for, active and peaceful. Despite their size, they can be kept with smaller fish and are good community tankmates for other active, robust fishes.

WHAT size?
Males and females 30cm.

WHAT does it eat?
Flake when young; pellet, live or frozen foods when adult.

WHERE is it from?
Large and medium-sized rivers and lakes in Southeast Asia.

WHAT does it cost?
★★☆☆☆ ★★★☆☆
Prices vary depending on size. Some large (15cm+) specimens are available, but should not be too costly.

Balantiocheilus melanopterus
Silver shark

HOW do I sex it?
Virtually impossible, although females in breeding condition are more rounded.

WHAT kind of tank?
Community aquarium.

WHAT minimum size tank?
150x60x60cm.

WHAT kind of water?
Adapts to a wide range of conditions.

HOW warm?
22-28°C.

WHAT decor?
Large, robust plants, hiding spots in bogwood or caves, plus plenty of open swimming space.

WHAT area of the tank?
All levels.

HOW many in one tank?
Keep in groups of three or more.

▲ *Their well-defined markings and sleek appearance make these fish a popular choice, although few fishkeepers have an aquarium large enough to house them.*

HOW does it behave?
Peaceful and active open-water swimmer.

WILL it breed in an aquarium?
Unlikely.

Botia lohachata
Pakistani loach

FISH PROFILE

The mischievous Pakistani loach has plenty of character. Its markings are both stunning and extremely variable, sometimes appearing as three Y shapes with spots inbetween, giving the fish its other common name of yo-yo loach. On other, and particularly older, specimens the markings appear less bold and more mazelike. Tankmates for these fish should be of a robust nature, as weaker, quieter fish can be harassed. As with other loaches, these fish seem to be at their best when kept in shoals, rather than as individuals or in small groups.

WHAT size?
Males and females 12cm.

WHAT does it eat?
Sinking foods; pellets, wafers, live and frozen foods.

WHERE is it from?
Asia; usually found in pools, streams and rivers with rocky or gravel substrates.

WHAT does it cost?
★★☆☆☆ ★★★☆☆
For an attractively patterned fish, these loaches are well priced. Many retailers offer discounts for group purchases.

HOW do I sex it?
No known visual external differences.

WHAT kind of tank?
Community with no delicate or slow fishes.

WHAT minimum size tank?
90x30x30cm.

WHAT kind of water?
Will adapt to most water conditions.

HOW warm?
24-28°C.

▼ *The distinctive patterns on these young specimens will change as the fish mature.*

WHAT decor?
Provide a smooth or sandy substrate and hiding spots amongst plants, wood or caves.

WHAT area of the tank?
Bottom level.

HOW many in one tank?
Best kept either singly or in larger groups of four or more.

HOW does it behave?
Generally peaceful and active, but individuals can harass other fish and some adults will fight.

WILL it breed in an aquarium?
Unlikely.

Botia sidthimunki

Dwarf chain loach

FISH PROFILE

This is one of the smallest loaches and ideal for a peaceful community aquarium. It is adaptable, active during the day, and scavenges the aquarium substrate for food items. Although a very useful aquarium fish, it is seasonal and may only be offered for sale at certain times of the year. Feeding a wide variety of foods and providing a few hiding spots will keep it in first-class health.

WHAT size?
Males and females up to 6cm.

WHAT does it eat?
Omnivorous. Offer a mixture of sinking pellets, wafers, live or frozen foods. May learn to take flake food from the surface.

WHERE is it from?
Muddy-bottomed pools, rivers, streams and flooded regions in Northern India and Thailand.

WHAT does it cost?
★★★☆☆ ★★★★★
More expensive in recent years.

HOW do I sex it?
No known visual external differences.

WHAT kind of tank?
Community aquarium with other peaceful and active fish.

WHAT minimum size tank?
60x30x30cm.

WHAT kind of water?
Will adapt to a wide range of water conditions.

HOW warm?
25-28°C.

WHAT decor?
Small, smooth substrates will prevent damage to the fish's barbels. A well-planted lower region, with plenty of hiding spots and dark areas will be appreciated.

WHAT area of the tank?
Middle, bottom and on all surfaces.

HOW many in one tank?
These very sociable fish are best kept in groups of three or more.

HOW does it behave?
Peaceful and active during the day.

WILL it breed in an aquarium?
Unlikely; the fish are seasonal, suggesting they do not normally breed in an aquarium.

▼ *Dwarf chain loaches are better suited to small communities than most loaches. Their constant scavenging will help to remove snails and debris.*

Botia striata

Zebra loach

Of all the loach group, the zebra loach is one of the best suited to the aquarium. It is ideal for a community set-up, where its active and playful nature makes it an interesting and welcome addition. Zebra loaches are very sociable and need to be kept in groups. Because of their constant scavenging activity, a soft substrate is essential to protect their sensitive barbels. In the wild these fish feed on a wide range of small aquatic creatures, and a varied diet in the aquarium of both dried and frozen or live foods will help to keep them in optimum health.

▲ *Impressive markings, an active nature and a manageable size make the zebra loach a popular aquarium fish.*

WHAT size?
  Males and females 10cm.

WHAT does it eat?
  Sinking dried foods, supplemented with frozen or live foods.

WHERE is it from?
  Southern India; found in both clear mountain streams and muddy waterways.

WHAT does it cost?
  ★★☆☆☆ ★★★☆☆
  Readily available; price may reflect differences in size.

HOW do I sex it?
  No known visual external differences.

WHAT kind of tank?
  Community, avoiding very delicate or slow species.

WHAT minimum size tank?
  75x30x30cm.

WHAT kind of water?
  Adaptable, but avoid very hard water over the longer term.

HOW warm?
  24-26°C.

WHAT decor?
  A sandy or smooth substrate is essential. Provide hiding spots amongst rocks, wood and plants.

WHAT area of the tank?
  Bottom level.

HOW many in one tank?
  Keep in groups of at least three.

HOW does it behave?
  Peaceful, active and lively.

WILL it breed in an aquarium?
  Unlikely.

Chromobotia macracanthus

Clown loach

FISH PROFILE

The bold markings and active nature of the clown loach have made it one of the most popular aquarium fish of recent times. As it grows up to 20cm in the aquarium, a group of adults will require a large tank. Provide either a sandy or smooth substrate so that these scavengers do not damage their sensitive barbels. Hiding spots are also important, as they can be quite scatty and timid at times and retreats will encourage confidence. Established individuals are active and lively, making them excellent tankmates for other robust fishes.

WHAT size?
Males and females 20cm in the aquarium, larger in the wild.

WHAT does it eat?
Sinking pellet foods, catfish foods, live or frozen foods. Provide a varied diet for optimum health.

WHERE is it from?
Asia; moving and standing waters around vegetation.

WHAT does it cost?
★★★☆☆ ★★★★☆
Prices remain high due to breeding difficulties and strong demand.

HOW do I sex it?
Difficult to sex; females are thinner; males may have elongated caudal (tail) fins.

WHAT kind of tank?
Community aquarium with other robust fishes.

WHAT minimum size tank?
120x45x45cm.

WHAT kind of water?
Prefers soft water, but will adapt to medium-hard water; pH6.5-8.

HOW warm?
24-28°C.

▼ *Few freshwater fish can boast such bright and well-defined colours as the clown loach.*

WHAT decor?
Provide hiding spots amongst roots and caves, plus a sandy or smooth, rounded substrate. Robust plants can be included.

WHAT area of the tank?
Bottom level.

HOW many in one tank?
Must be kept in groups of at least three, ideally five or more.

HOW does it behave?
Active, peaceful and playful, sometimes boisterous. As with other loaches, these fish may spend periods resting on their sides.

WILL it breed in an aquarium?
Aquarium spawnings have been reported but are very rare.

177

Crossocheilus siamensis

Siamese flying fox

FISH PROFILE

The Siamese flying fox may not be the most colourful aquarium fish, but it is certainly one of the most useful. It is an excellent algae-eater, even tackling the fibrous hair and brush algae that most other algae-eaters leave behind. And having an active nature, these fish make excellent tankmates for other sizeable, robust fishes. Identifying the Siamese flying fox can be difficult, as a number of very similar-looking fish are available in the hobby, but none of these relations will be as effective at clearing algae, and some can be troublesome in a community aquarium.

WHAT size?
Males and females 15cm.

WHAT does it eat?
Algae, sinking foods, vegetable matter, frozen and live foods.

WHERE is it from?
Rivers, streams and flooded areas in Southeast Asia.

WHAT does it cost?
★☆☆☆☆   ★★☆☆☆
A good supply of this relatively drab fish keeps prices low. However, this species is worth much more than its actual cost for its useful algae-eating habits.

HOW do I sex it?
No known visual external differences.

WHAT kind of tank?
Community aquarium with medium-sized to large fish.

WHAT minimum size tank?
90x45x45cm.

WHAT kind of water?
Very adaptable to a wide range of conditions.

HOW warm?
18-24°C.

WHAT decor?
Needs hiding spots amongst vegetation and bogwood, otherwise undemanding.

WHAT area of the tank?
Bottom, middle and on the surfaces of tank decor.

▼ *A tendency to eat hair algae makes this fish an indispensable addition to the aquarium.*

HOW many in one tank?
Can be kept singly or in groups.

HOW does it behave?
This peaceful, active species spends most of its time feeding from the surface of tank decor, plants and the glass. An excellent aquarium fish.

WILL it breed in an aquarium?
Not known.

Epalzeorhynchos bicolor
Red-tailed black shark

FISH PROFILE

This well-known aquarium fish often delivers the first lesson in compatibility experienced by the fishkeeper. When young, it is active, shoaling, peaceful and full of character, but within a few months the mature fish quickly becomes an aggressive, territorial bully. However, with the right tankmates, an adult red-tail can be a great addition to the aquarium. It has a strong personality, is tough and adaptable, and with good care, exhibits a stunning solid body shape and colour.

WHAT size?
Males and females 12cm.

WHAT does it eat?
Sinking foods and algae wafers, supplemented with a variety of live or frozen foods.

WHERE is it from?
Although it originates in Asia, the fish may now be completely extinct in the wild, partly due to collection for aquariums, but mainly because of the destruction of its natural habitats. All stocks for sale are captive-bred.

WHAT does it cost?
★★☆☆☆
This fish was once far more popular than it is now. Improved advice means that more fishkeepers are aware of its aggressive nature. Reduced demand keeps prices down.

▲ *With its jet-black body, bright red tail and a 'sharklike' dorsal fin, even a single specimen is hard to miss.*

HOW do I sex it?
Difficult to sex; the male's dorsal fin may be more pointed.

WHAT kind of tank?
Best kept in a community of tough, large and robust tankmates.

WHAT minimum size tank?
120x45x45cm.

WHAT kind of water?
Undemanding, will easily adapt to a wide range of conditions.

HOW warm?
22-26°C.

WHAT decor?
Provide a few hiding spots under bogwood or in caves. The fish sometimes use items of decor to establish territorial boundaries.

WHAT area of the tank?
A bottom-dweller, but will explore the surfaces of tank decor.

HOW many in one tank?
Best kept singly unless housed in a very large aquarium. Small numbers will result in one individual becoming a dominant bully.

HOW does it behave?
Territorial and aggressive towards its own kind and closely related fish. Will chase and bully weaker or timid fish to the point of death, but can be kept with other robust species, such as medium-sized to large barbs, rainbowfishes and cichlids.

WILL it breed in an aquarium?
Unlikely.

Epalzeorhynchos frenatum

Ruby shark

FISH PROFILE

The ruby shark is a good alternative to the red-tail black shark for a community aquarium with less robust tankmates. Although rubys will squabble with each other and closely related fish, they usually leave other fish alone and are not aggressively territorial. As the fish ages, its black body colour may fade slightly, but with proper care and feeding, a well-established ruby shark can become a very attractive aquarium fish. Although it is a good algae-eater, a large ruby may damage some delicate foliage, so choose robust plant species for the aquarium. Avoid buying malnourished or thin individuals. An albino variety is available.

WHAT size?
Males and females 15cm.

WHAT does it eat?
Provide a varied diet that includes sinking pellets, algae wafers, live and frozen foods. A natural algae-grazer.

WHERE is it from?
Asia; mainly found in tributaries and flooded regions in the Mekong River Basin.

WHAT does it cost?
★★☆☆☆
Relatively inexpensive. Larger, more costly specimens are occasionally available.

HOW do I sex it?
Difficult to sex; males are thinner, with a darker anal fin.

WHAT kind of tank?
Community aquarium with robust tankmates.

WHAT minimum size tank?
90x45x45cm.

WHAT kind of water?
Undemanding.

HOW warm?
24-26°C.

WHAT decor?
Provide a few hiding spots under roots or in caves.

▲ *A varied diet will ensure that young specimens mature with strong colours and a good body shape.*

WHAT area of the tank?
Bottom, on the surfaces of decor.

HOW many in one tank?
Best kept singly or in groups of four or more.

HOW does it behave?
Relatively peaceful and active, although it will squabble with its own kind and closely related species.

WILL it breed in an aquarium?
Unlikely.

Epalzeorhynchos kallopterus

Flying fox

FISH PROFILE

The flying fox is readily available and often acquired by mistake in place of the Siamese flying fox. Although it will eat some algae, it will not touch hair algae, unlike the Siamese flying fox. Flying foxes are solitary fish that become territorial with age, so only keep one per tank. Delicate or quiet tankmates may be harassed, so flying foxes are better suited to communities of larger barbs, rainbowfish and cichlids. Provide a varied diet and good filtration to ensure long-term health.

WHAT size?
Males and females 15cm.

WHAT does it eat?
A scavenger and algae-eater; provide a variety of dried sinking foods and live or frozen foods.

WHERE is it from?
Asia; occurs in flowing waters.

WHAT does it cost?
★☆☆☆☆
Inexpensive and widely available.

HOW do I sex it?
No known visual external differences.

WHAT kind of tank?
Best kept in a community of tough, robust fishes, with no closely related fish.

WHAT minimum size tank?
90x45x45cm.

WHAT kind of water?
Prefers slightly soft and acidic water, but is adaptable.

HOW warm?
24-26°C.

WHAT decor?
Provide rocks and hiding spots in caves or under bogwood; broadleaved and robust plants are also appreciated.

WHAT area of the tank?
Bottom, and on the surfaces of tank decor.

HOW many in one tank?
Best kept singly.

HOW does it behave?
Territorial and aggressive; will constantly fight with closely related fish, but will not bother other robust species.

WILL it breed in an aquarium?
Unlikely.

▲ *The flying fox is a lively and robust addition to the aquarium, but choose its tankmates with care.*

Misgurnis anguillicaudatus

Chinese weatherfish

FISH PROFILE

The Chinese weatherfish is very similar to the once popular weather loach. However, it is now illegal to import the weather loach without a licence. The unusual Chinese weatherfish has plenty of behavioural attributes that make it a good addition to the aquarium. Measuring up to 20cm, potentially more, it will require a good-sized tank, with a soft or sandy substrate in which to burrow. During the day, it remains mostly hidden, often with its head poking up above the substrate, and only becomes active during feeding periods and at night.

WHAT size?
Males and females normally up to 20cm in the aquarium. There are reports of wild fish measuring up to 50cm.

WHAT does it eat?
Scavenger; will take any sinking foods. Offer a varied diet with dried and plenty of live or frozen foods.

WHERE is it from?
Rivers, lakes, swamps and ponds with muddy or debris-covered bottoms in Asia.

WHAT does it cost?
★★☆☆☆   ★★★☆☆
Relatively new on the market, so prices may vary.

HOW do I sex it?
Difficult. Males may have thicker dorsal fin rays.

WHAT kind of tank?
Temperate or cool tropical community aquarium.

WHAT minimum size tank?
90x45x30cm.

WHAT kind of water?
Undemanding, will adapt to most conditions.

HOW warm?
10-25°C. Can be kept in an unheated aquarium, but not with delicate fancy goldfish, which may be harassed.

WHAT decor?
A soft sand or fine, smooth substrate is vital, since the fish likes to burrow and has delicate barbels. It appreciates a few hiding spots under decor and/or plants.

WHAT area of the tank?
Bottom level.

HOW many in one tank?
One or more. Not a grouping fish.

HOW does it behave?
Peaceful and active during dusk, dawn and feeding times. Some behaviours are amusing. Undemanding and adaptable.

WILL it breed in an aquarium?
Unlikely.

▲ *Chinese weatherfish are excellent scavengers for unheated tanks. Take care that the fishes' delicate barbels are not damaged.*

Pangio kuhlii
Kuhli loach

FISH PROFILE

The Kuhli loach's unusual, wormlike appearance and swimming patterns account in part for its popularity. In sales tanks it swims actively and buries itself in the substrate. This lively behaviour is often simply the result of a lack of hiding spots; once in a home community aquarium, it remains hidden away most of the time, making only occasional appearances at feeding times. A few pattern variations are available and an entirely black variety has become popular in recent years.

WHAT size?
Males and females 12cm.

WHAT does it eat?
Provide this scavenger and bottom-feeder with sinking and small frozen foods.

WHERE is it from?
A range of stream, river and pond habitats in Southeast Asia.

WHAT does it cost?
★☆☆☆☆
Inexpensive. Colour varieties may cost more.

HOW do I sex it?
No known visual external differences.

WHAT kind of tank?
Community aquarium.

WHAT minimum size tank?
60x30x30cm.

WHAT kind of water?
Best kept in soft to medium-hard water, pH up to 7.5.

HOW warm?
24-28°C.

WHAT decor?
Combine small, smooth-particle or sandy substrates with hiding spots and vegetation along the lower areas of the tank.

▲ *Kuhlis are well suited to aquarium life, providing they have plenty of hiding spots and soft or rounded substrates.*

WHAT area of the tank?
Bottom level.

HOW many in one tank?
Although the fish will group, they are natural loners and can be kept singly.

HOW does it behave?
Peaceful and reclusive, but active during feeding times; a burrower.

WILL it breed in an aquarium?
Difficult to breed.

183

Nature's weird and wonderful

▶ Many of the species we call oddballs today were around when the dinosaurs roamed the earth, well over 200 million years ago. Fish such as the polypterus, lungfishes, snakeheads and gars all possess an accessory, or secondary, breathing organ that allows them to survive times of drought. These organs enable the fish to take in atmospheric air by gulping at the surface. Other good examples are the many species of knifefishes that effectively stalk their prey by producing a weak electrical field around their bodies.

Others, such as the South American leaf fish, lie in wait, perfectly camouflaged amongst real leaves, for their unfortunate victims to come along. The list is almost endless and fascinating to those of us who are always on the lookout for something out of the ordinary. The species featured here are just some of the favourites that you can find.

Price guide

★	Less than £5
★★	£6 – 10
★★★	£12 – 15
★★★★	£20 – 30
★★★★★	£75 +

This fish is without doubt one of the weirdest species to come out of South America. However, it has a very gentle nature, making it a popular choice for the larger aquarium. You will never tire of watching this graceful fish parading in its tank, using its undulating, elongated anal fin.

▶ *These side and bottom views clearly show the rippling motion of the elongated anal fin that powers this extraordinary fish through the water.*

WHAT size?
40-50cm in the wild, but captive-raised specimens (males and females) seldom grow larger than 25-30cm.

WHAT does it eat?
Bloodworm, earthworms, chopped mussels, cockles, sinking pellets and flake food.

WHERE is it from?
Venezuela, Guyana and Peru, as well as Brazil.

WHAT does it cost?
★★★☆☆
Once quite expensive, but large numbers have been imported over the past few years, bringing the prices tumbling down. This price rating is for a 15cm fish.

Apteronotus albifrons

Black ghost knifefish

HOW do I sex it?
No visual external differences.

WHAT kind of tank?
Large fish community. Provide subdued illumination.

WHAT minimum size tank?
100x45x38cm.

WHAT kind of water?
A mature aquarium is vital. Prefers soft to medium-hard water and pH6.8-7, although this is not critical.

HOW warm?
23-28°C.

WHAT decor?
Bogwood and clay pipes amongst dense planting.

WHAT area of the tank?
Usually middle to bottom, but frequently reaches the surface for food.

HOW many in one tank?
One, or a group of three or more.

▲ *Not a pretty face, but a fish with endless appeal and a gentle disposition.*

HOW does it behave?
Rarely seen when kept alone. Fish are far more conspicuous when part of a large group that engages in continuous territorial disputes. These rarely amount to anything more than the odd frayed fin or two.

WILL it breed in an aquarium?
Although not a common occurrence, it has been known to spawn in a medium-sized aquarium. Keeping several individuals together and providing them with caves and crevices appear to be the keys to breeding success.

Channa micropeltes

Red snakehead

FISH PROFILE

Do not be fooled by this fish's attractive juvenile appearance. This bruiser grows into one of the most unpredictable, aggressive predators ever kept in either a domestic or public aquarium. This species is not for the faint-hearted; it is extremely powerful and a bite from one could result in a wound requiring a few stitches.

WHAT size?
Females 90cm (larger in the wild). Males tend to be slightly smaller.

WHAT does it eat?
Most fresh or frozen meaty foods, including beef heart, sprats, mussels and squid. Rarely accepts dry food.

WHERE is it from?
India to western Malaysia.

WHAT does it cost?
★★☆☆☆
Far too many are imported each year and sold to unsuspecting aquarists. Its low price tag does nothing to deter customers. This price rating is for a 10cm fish.

HOW do I sex it?
Juveniles are impossible to sex. Adult females tend to be thicker around the girth.

WHAT kind of tank?
Species aquarium.

WHAT minimum size tank?
180x90x60cm.

WHAT kind of water?
This hardy species adapts to most types of water, but avoid extremes.

HOW warm?
25-28°C.

WHAT decor?
Keep decor to a minimum. A few large, smooth boulders and bogwood on a 6mm pea gravel substrate.

WHAT area of the tank?
An active fish that utilises the whole of the tank.

HOW many in one tank?
Keep singly.

HOW does it behave?
This intelligent eating machine often remains motionless in midwater, fully aware of what is happening around it.

WILL it breed in an aquarium?
Given its eventual size, aquarium breeding is out of the question.

▲ *This sub-adult specimen has already lost its juvenile coloration.*

Chitala chitala
Clown knifefish

FISH PROFILE

Juveniles display very little in the way of eyespots – inconspicuous tiny dots would be a fairer description. However, as they mature, the pattern develops to make it one of the most spectacular oddballs.

WHAT size?
In the wild, 100cm; in the aquarium, males and females 60cm.

WHAT does it eat?
Bloodworm, earthworms, prawns, mussels and cockles, lancefish. High-protein pelleted food.

▼ *Bold eyespots create a distinctive pattern along the flanks of the fish.*

WHERE is it from?
Thailand and Burma.

WHAT does it cost?
★★☆☆☆
Rating for a 13cm fish. Very affordable for an unusual fish.

HOW do I sex it?
No external sex differences. Gravid (egg-carrying) females appear heavier during the breeding season.

WHAT kind of tank?
Specialist community aquarium.

WHAT minimum size tank?
120x60x60cm for a single specimen.

WHAT kind of water?
Ideally soft, pH6-6.5. Will adapt to most types of water, but avoid extremes.

HOW warm?
24-28°C.

WHAT decor?
A well-planted tank, with bogwood and smooth boulders to provide essential cover, but leave enough open swimming space.

▲ *Do not be fooled by the apparent smile on this predator's face.*

WHAT area of the tank?
Middle, with frequent visits to the surface for air.

HOW many in one tank?
Providing they are all acquired at the same time, a group of three or more. However, some individuals need to be housed alone, due to their aggressive nature.

HOW does it behave?
Mainly peaceful when kept with other large fishes, but highly predatory towards any fish small enough to fit into its huge mouth.

WILL it breed in an aquarium?
Rarely. The male cares for the eggs and fry.

187

Erpetoichthys calabaricus

Reedfish, ropefish

FISH PROFILE

The snakelike appearance of this fish never fails to create interest, particularly amongst children. Reedfish are hardy and easy to keep once established. Unfortunately, however, many newly imported specimens perish before they reach retail aquatic outlets.

Is it a reptile or is it a fish? The similarities are there for all to see. The tube nostrils are sensory organs that perform the same function as the barbels of catfish.

WHAT size?
Males and females 40cm.

WHAT does it eat?
Sinking pellets, chopped fish, bloodworm, earthworms, prawns, cockles, etc. A real scavenger.

WHERE is it from?
Nigeria and Cameroon.

WHAT does it cost?
★★☆☆☆
At such a low price, even acquiring a small group is feasible.

HOW do I sex it?
Females have nine anal fin rays, whereas males have 12 to 14.

WHAT kind of tank?
Community tank housing medium-sized to large fishes.

WHAT minimum size tank?
75x45x30cm.

WHAT kind of water?
Medium-hard, neutral to alkaline (pH7-7.8).

HOW warm?
22-28°C.

WHAT decor?
A well-planted tank with numerous hiding places in the shape of bogwood, boulders and clay pipes. Sand or fine gravel substrate.

WHAT area of the tank?
A bottom-dweller that frequently breaks the water surface to take in atmospheric air.

HOW many in one tank?
As many as the tank will comfortably support.

HOW does it behave?
A slow-moving, non-aggressive fish that often appears quite dopey, particularly at feeding time. Food must literally touch its nose before it finally feeds.

WILL it breed in an aquarium?
There have been rare reports of captive breeding. On one occasion it was triggered by reducing the water level to about 15cm and raising the temperature to 30°C for a considerable time, before finally lowering it by gently trickling in cool water using a hosepipe.

Gobioides broussonnetii

Violet, or dragon, goby

FISH PROFILE

This species would not look out of place in a scary undersea movie. However, despite its terrifying appearance, it is in fact very placid and does well in a community situation with medium-sized fishes. Small specimens measuring about 13cm are even safe with small fish such as tetras.

WHAT size?
Males and females 20cm in captivity, although wild specimens are said to reach much more than this.

WHAT does it eat?
Small foods, such as daphnia, brineshrimp and bloodworm. Will even take flake and pellets on occasion.

WHERE is it from?
The Americas: Georgia south to Brazil.

WHAT does it cost?
★★★☆☆
Unfortunately, this fish only appears amongst shipments in the trade two or three times a year.

▼ *A top view clearly shows the snake-like appearance of this fish.*

HOW do I sex it?
In many fish of this genus, the males are said to have a flattened genital papilla, but this characteristic is not so evident in this species.

WHAT kind of tank?
Community aquarium.

WHAT minimum size tank?
90x38x38cm for a single specimen should suffice, since the violet goby is unlikely to grow very large.

WHAT kind of water?
Soft, slightly acidic to neutral (pH6.5-7). Fresh or slightly brackish.

HOW warm?
23-25°C.

WHAT decor?
Rocks, caves and driftwood. Appreciates a sandy substrate, as it likes to burrow.

WHAT area of the tank?
Bottom-dweller.

HOW many in one tank?
One in a 90cm tank. If you intend keeping more than one, this territorial species will need a sizeable aquarium with plenty of caves.

HOW does it behave?
The head of this slow-moving species moves from side-to-side, independently of its body. With its gaping mouth and gulping action, it quietly but efficiently goes about its business as a filter-feeder.

WILL it breed in an aquarium?
Never knowingly bred in a home aquarium.

▼ *The expression 'never judge a book by its cover' takes on a whole new meaning with this species.*

Gnathonemus petersi

Elephantnose

FISH PROFILE

A delicate fish that requires a little more dedication on the part of the fishkeeper if it is to thrive long term. Since it does not compete heavily for food, a busy community aquarium is totally unsuitable for this timid species.

WHAT size?
Males and females 20cm.

WHAT does it eat?
Bloodworm, glassworm, daphnia, cyclops and brineshrimp.

WHERE is it from?
Zaire, Nigeria and Cameroon.

WHAT does it cost?
★★☆☆☆
Reasonably priced.

HOW do I sex it?
The male's anal fin is concave on the lower edge.

WHAT kind of tank?
Specialist community.

WHAT minimum size tank?
90x30x38cm.

WHAT kind of water?
Ideally, soft, slightly acidic (pH6.5-6.8), although it will tolerate higher pH levels.

HOW warm?
20-26°C.

WHAT decor?
Densely planted, with plenty of caves to create essential cover.

WHAT area of the tank?
Bottom to middle.

Mouth

HOW many in one tank?
A gregarious species, best kept in groups of six or more.

HOW does it behave?
Peaceful towards other species, but regularly participates in territorial disputes amongst its own group. However, this is a method of communication and never results in physical damage.

WILL it breed in an aquarium?
Never knowingly bred in captivity.

▼ *Although similar in appearance to G. petersi, this is a different species, namely* Campylomormyrus tamandua. *Both species require the same care in the aquarium.*

◀ *In G. petersi, the mouth can be clearly seen at the beginning of the trunk, positioned not far from the nostril.*

Mouth

▶ *Note the slope of the head and position of the mouth. The floppy appendage (trunk) is no more than 5mm away from the mouth opening in this species.*

Mastacembelus erythrotaenia

Fire eel

Unquestionably the prettiest of the spiny eel group, albeit rather a large fish. Specimens measuring more than 75cm have been kept with fish as small as 8cm without any form of molestation or predation taking place. Fire eels are real characters that become very tame in captivity.

WHAT size?
Up to 120cm in the wild, but females rarely exceed 75cm in the aquarium, males slightly smaller.

WHAT does it eat?
Earthworms, prawns, cockles, krill and bloodworm.

WHERE is it from?
Thailand, Sumatra and Borneo.

WHAT does it cost?
★★★☆☆
The price rating is for juveniles measuring 15cm; expect to pay substantially more for a 30cm specimen.

HOW do I sex it?
Adult females are somewhat heavier and thicker than the smaller males.

WHAT kind of tank?
Large community aquarium.

WHAT minimum size tank?
150x60x60cm.

WHAT kind of water?
Medium-hard, neutral to slightly alkaline (pH7-7.5). Adding one teaspoon of salt per 4.5 litres of water can benefit this species.

HOW warm?
23-28°C.

WHAT decor?
Loves the security of a clay or plastic pipe. Include smooth boulders and bogwood on a substrate that is not too sharp. The fire eel has a habit of burying itself, and its skin is easily damaged.

WHAT area of the tank?
Bottom-dweller.

▲ *The dramatic markings are just part of the attraction of this lively fish. A real aquarium star.*

HOW many in one tank?
One. Although peaceful towards other tankmates, it does not take kindly to its own species.

HOW does it behave?
Sedentary, but can move with lightning speed when alarmed. Fit a tight lid to secure this expert escape artist.

WILL it breed in an aquarium?
Never knowingly bred in a home aquarium.

Osteoglossum bicirrhosum

Silver arowana

FISH PROFILE

The most common and affordable arowana available in the hobby. Although its Asian and Australian cousins of the genus *Scleropages* have a remarkably similar head shape, the body of this species is more elongated, with anal and dorsal fins that run almost its entire length. These predatory bony tongues, as they are sometimes called, have excellent eyesight that enables them to spot small insects crawling on the lower branches of overhanging trees. Adopting an S-shaped posture, they can fling themselves high into the trees to seize their prey.

WHAT size?
In the aquarium, females 75cm (males slightly smaller); larger in the wild.

WHAT does it eat?
Insects, beetles, mealworms, mussels, cockles. Floating foodsticks.

WHERE is it from?
Rio Negro and other areas of the Amazon.

WHAT does it cost?
★★★☆☆   ★★★★★
Price depends on size. Usually the cheapest arowana species.

HOW do I sex it?
Adult females are noticeably deeper-bodied. Males are said to have a slightly undershot jaw, although this is not absolutely certain.

WHAT kind of tank?
Large specialist community aquarium.

WHAT minimum size tank?
180x75x60cm.

WHAT kind of water?
Ideally, soft, slightly acidic to neutral (pH6.7-7). Will tolerate other types, but avoid extremes.

HOW warm?
24-30°C.

WHAT decor?
Soft sand substrate. Well-planted, with large beech branches, bogwood and smooth rockwork. (Use fallen beech branches that are dry, without rot and have lost their bark.)

WHAT area of the tank?
Surface-dweller.

HOW many in one tank?
One or groups of three or more.

▲ *The sleek menace of this ancient fish is truly fascinating for experienced fishkeepers. Only suitable for large tanks.*

HOW does it behave?
Generally peaceful towards other large species, but when kept in a group of its own kind, it is common to see superficial damage to the fins and body as a result of territorial disputes.

WILL it breed in an aquarium?
Yes, it has been bred on a commercial basis, but private captive breeding is less common. The male broods the eggs and fry until they can fend for themselves.

Pantodon buchholzi

Butterflyfish

FISH PROFILE

With its straight back, upturned mouth and wonderful camouflage, the rather weird-looking butterflyfish has all the qualities needed to be a very efficient predator of insects and small, surface-swimming fishes. Any fish too large to be considered bite-sized will almost certainly be left alone.

WHAT size?
Males and females 10cm.

WHAT does it eat?
Small brown crickets, mealworms and flies. Freeze-dried floating foods, as well as flake food.

WHERE is it from?
Nigeria, Cameroon, Zaire.

WHAT does it cost?
★★☆☆☆
Exotic but not expensive.

HOW do I sex it?
The male's anal fin has a convex curve on the trailing edge, whereas the female's anal fin is straight.

WHAT kind of tank?
Community aquarium housing similar-sized fishes.

WHAT minimum size tank?
60x30x30cm.

WHAT kind of water?
Soft, slightly acid (pH6.5-6.8).

HOW warm?
23-30°C.

WHAT decor?
Heavily planted, including surface cover, such as Amazon frogbit and floating fern (*Ceratopteris thalictroides*).

WHAT area of the tank?
Surface-dweller.

HOW many in one tank?
Small group of, say, three to six.

HOW does it behave?
Although peaceful towards other large fish, it often gets quarrelsome with any fish that tries to invade its space at the surface. Best kept with middle- to bottom-dwelling species.

WILL it breed in an aquarium?
Yes. The eggs float to the surface, where they can be easily removed to a rearing tank. Unfortunately, the fry of this specialist feeder are difficult to raise.

◀ ▼ *From these views it is easy to see how this species acquired its common name.*

Parambassis ranga

Indian glassfish

FISH PROFILE

The body is transparent, allowing you to see all the vital organs. Unfortunately, fish are sometimes injected with brightly coloured dye into the muscle tissue. Never buy such fish; not only do they look ridiculous, but this cruel practice also shortens their life.

WHAT size?
Males and females 8cm.

WHAT does it eat?
Daphnia, bloodworm, cyclops, brineshrimp and mysis.

WHERE is it from?
India, Thailand and Burma.

WHAT does it cost?
★☆☆☆☆
In common with many other Indian species, this glassfish is very reasonably priced compared with fish imported from other countries, notably South America.

▲ *Why alter such natural beauty? Any glassfish with gaudy coloration should be treated with suspicion.*

HOW do I sex it?
Males have a bright blue pencil-line edging to both the dorsal and anal fins. The swimbladder in males ends in a point.

WHAT kind of tank?
Community aquarium.

WHAT minimum size tank?
60x30x30cm.

WHAT kind of water?
Tolerates both fresh and brackish water; the latter is more favourable. The water should be hard, pH7-7.8, with a specific gravity of 1.010 if kept in brackish water.

HOW warm?
23-26°C.

WHAT decor?
A well-planted tank with many hideaways suits this nervous fish.

WHAT area of the tank?
Middle to lower levels.

HOW many in one tank?
A shoaling species, so keep a minimum of six.

HOW does it behave?
A slow-moving fish that prefers to stay motionless as part of a group in the middle of the tank. Introducing food will motivate it.

WILL it breed in an aquarium?
Yes, easy to breed, but raising the tiny fry is difficult. Spawning is triggered by an increase in temperature, and the adhesive eggs are caught in plant thickets. The fry become free-swimming within 48 hours.

Polypterus senegalensis

Bichir

FISH PROFILE

As proved by the many fossil remains found today, this group of fishes has barely changed in appearance for more than 200 million years. Many members of this genus make very interesting subjects for the oddball fanatic.

WHAT size?
Males and females 30cm.

WHAT does it eat?
Anything with a strong scent, such as chopped fish, mussels, prawns, worms, krill, as well as high-protein sinking pellets.

WHERE is it from?
Widespread throughout Africa, being found in Senegal, Gambia, Nigeria and Zaire.

WHAT does it cost?
★★☆☆☆ ★★★☆☆
Surprisingly inexpensive!

▼ The bichir is a fascinating example of a true living fossil. This is a juvenile specimen.

HOW do I sex it?
The male has a much broader anal fin, used to cradle the eggs during their fertilisation.

WHAT kind of tank?
Specialist community aquarium.

WHAT minimum size tank?
90x38x30cm.

WHAT kind of water?
Soft to medium-hard, neutral to slightly alkaline (pH7-7.5), but will adapt to most kinds of water.

HOW warm?
25-28°C.

WHAT decor?
Provide this inquisitive fish with plenty of caves and hideaways to explore. Clay pipes and bogwood are good choices.

WHAT area of the tank?
Bottom-dweller.

HOW many in one tank?
Given sufficient space, several will live together, but that is not to say that there won't be the occasional disagreement.

HOW does it behave?
Generally quite a steady character that rarely, if ever, molests other large fishes. Must have access to atmospheric air, otherwise, it will drown.

WILL it breed in an aquarium?
Yes, there have been numerous accounts of successful breeding. The male catches the eggs using his modified anal fin, and they are fertilised here before being deposited among plant thickets or rocks.

▲ The amazing pectoral fins resemble table tennis bats – they are typical of this group of fishes. The tube nostrils are used to locate prey during the night.

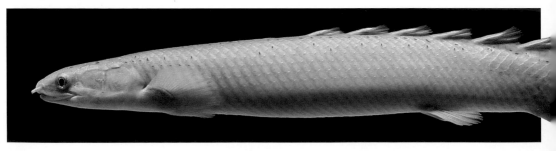

Potamotrygon motoro

Common freshwater stingray

FISH PROFILE

Contrary to popular belief, this fascinating fish is not difficult to keep. It becomes very friendly, even to the point of taking food from its owner's hand – but plastic tongs are safer!

WHAT size?
Disc size 60cm.

WHAT does it eat?
Bloodworm, earthworms, prawns, cockles, mussels, river shrimp and lancefish.

WHERE is it from?
Peru, Brazil and Colombia.

WHAT does it cost?
★★★★★
Affordable member of the genus.

▶ *Although extremely variable in pattern and coloration, this morph is the one most often encountered and typical of the species.*

HOW do I sex it?
Males have modified pelvic fins called claspers (as do their close relatives, the sharks). These are visible from birth.

WHAT kind of tank?
Specialist community aquarium.

WHAT minimum size tank?
180x60x60cm.

WHAT kind of water?
Closely match that of the supplier before buying this surprisingly adaptable fish. Avoid extremes.

HOW warm?
23-25°C.

WHAT decor?
Large-grain sand, no more than 2.5cm deep, smooth pebbles and driftwood. Decorate the tank as sparsely as possible, leaving the fish a generous amount of swimming space.

WHAT area of the tank?
Bottom, but regularly ventures up the sides of the aquarium.

HOW many in one tank?
Two females and one male if the tank is large enough.

HOW does it behave?
Becomes very active once acclimatised. An enthusiastic feeder that constantly pounds the sand in search of tasty morsels.

WILL it breed in an aquarium?
Yes. This species has reproduced in captivity more than any other stingray. Females give birth to live young that soon learn to fend for themselves. Feed the young on live bloodworm as a starter food.

Tateurndina ocellicauda

Peacock goby

FISH PROFILE

Not many unusual fish, particularly in the goby family, are suitable for a general community tank. However, this one is; it has a peaceful disposition and is without a shadow of a doubt, one of the most beautiful little sleeper gobies to grace the aquarium hobby.

▶ *This beautiful little species belies the theory that freshwater fish are no match for their marine counterparts.*

WHAT size?
Males 7.5cm, females usually smaller.

WHAT does it eat?
Prefers live foods, such as daphnia, brineshrimp, etc., but most frozen foods make good substitutes.

WHERE is it from?
East Papua, New Guinea.

WHAT does it cost?
★★☆☆☆
Once quite expensive for such a small fish, but prices have come down as a result of successful spawnings in captivity. This price rating is for a pair.

HOW do I sex it?
Males are larger, with a very round, bulky head and a flat ventral area. Females have a rounded abdomen and shorter dorsal and anal fins. In the females, these have a bright yellow fringe; in males, the fringe is paler. The photograph shows a female with the typical yellow-fringed fins and fuller belly area.

WHAT kind of tank?
Community aquarium.

WHAT minimum size tank?
45x30x30cm.

WHAT kind of water?
Prefers soft, neutral to very slightly alkaline water (pH7-7.2).

HOW warm?
22-26°C.

WHAT decor?
A densely planted aquarium with plenty of caves for spawning.

WHAT area of the tank?
Bottom to middle levels.

HOW many in one tank?
Single pair or large groups. To house a group of, say, 4 males to 10 females, upgrade the minimum tank size significantly.

HOW does it behave?
Generally peaceful as part of a mixed community tank, but can become a little territorial at spawning time.

WILL it breed in an aquarium?
Yes. Caves and crevices make ideal spawning sites. Both parents prepare the area, but once the eggs are deposited, the male chases away the female and tends the eggs himself.

Tetraodon miurus

Potato, or Congo box, puffer

FISH PROFILE

This little fellow can be – and usually is – a nasty piece of work, to say the least! However, due to its bizarre, some say cute, appearance, it finds a place in the heart – and tank – of many aquarists.

WHAT size?
Males and females 15cm (usually smaller in captivity).

WHAT does it eat?
Earthworms, small chopped frozen fish, mealworms, cockles, prawns and mussels. In most puffer species, the upturned mouth is designed for eating snails, but in the potato puffer its purpose is to ambush small fishes.

WHERE is it from?
Central and lower Congo.

WHAT does it cost?
★★★★☆
Not cheap, but well worth the expense.

HOW do I sex it?
No visual external differences.

WHAT kind of tank?
Species aquarium.

WHAT minimum size tank?
60x30x30cm.

WHAT kind of water?
Medium to soft, pH6.5-7.

HOW warm?
24-28°C.

WHAT decor?
Planted. Provide boulders, bogwood and a sand or fine gravel substrate, as these puffers like to bury themselves.

WHAT area of the tank?
Bottom to middle.

HOW many in one tank?
One. It is aggressive towards its own kind.

HOW does it behave?
Spends much of its time motionless on the bottom, although responsive at mealtimes.

WILL it breed in an aquarium?
No. How do you breed a fish in the confines of a tank when all it wants to do is kill its partner?

▼ *Without doubt, this is a species for the enthusiast. If you are after an active fish, look elsewhere.*

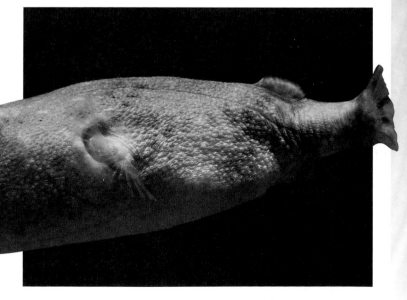

Starting out

▶ When it comes to buying fish, you must be satisfied that they are coming from an outlet that sells good-quality, really healthy stock. It is worth visiting all your local retailers to compare the quality and price of fish. Try to visit aquatic shops midweek when business is fairly quiet and the staff have more time to discuss your needs. Remember that it is in the retailer's interest to look after customers, whatever their level of knowledge. If you are unsure about the suitability of a fish, seek the dealer's advice – and if he can't help, ask him to reserve the fish while you do more research. If you are new to fishkeeping, start with easily maintained, farm-bred community species, such as small barbs, danios and tetras. These will build your confidence to try something more challenging. Most specialist fishkeepers learned the basic skills with a community tank before moving forward.

▶ *The red wag swordtail is an active, colourful livebearer.*

HOW do I choose a reliable aquatic dealer?
The retailer should have a licence to sell live animals and be a member of an aquatic trade association with rules on keeping its livestock. Look at the shop; is it clean? Are all the tanks clean, inside and out? There should be no dead or diseased fish on show. Never buy an apparently healthy fish from an aquarium containing diseased fish; the chances are that all the fish will be affected. Ideally, fish in quarantine should not be on view. All the tanks should have labels with details of the fish they contain and useful information regarding their price, potential size, special dietary or water requirements, compatibility, etc.

WHAT should I look for in a healthy fish?
Healthy fish deport well, swimming in a way typical of their species. The eyes should be clear, neither protuberant nor sunken; dorsal fins should be erect and other finnage carried clear of the body, with no serious splits, reddening or fraying. Missing or raised scales should alert you to potential problems. Fish that pass this visual check may have diseases that have yet to show themselves, but it makes sense to start with specimens that manifest no outward problems.

▲ *Look carefully at the dealer's tanks and do not buy fish on impulse.*

CAN I ask a dealer to select a particular fish?

It is reasonable to specify individual fish if you want a pair or if some are obviously larger or showing better colour than others of the same species. But do not expect shop staff to net, say, individual neon tetras for you from a tank that may contain hundreds of virtually identical specimens. It is not only impossible, but also stressful to the fish if the catcher attempts it.

HOW can I be sure of buying fish of both sexes?

If you are buying immature shoaling fish with no obvious external sexual differences, but want males and females with a view to spawning them later, a group of half a dozen will give you a better than 90 percent chance of obtaining both sexes.

WHAT if the colours of the dealer's fish are muted?

The colours of fish on sale may appear 'washed out' compared to the pictures in books and magazines. This is not necessarily a cause for concern. Many sales tanks are brightly lit and sparsely furnished, with no substrate. Fish show their best coloration against a darkish substrate and when refuges are available to them.

SHOULD I buy wild-caught fish for my aquarium?

Wild-caught fish are tempting buys, usually being larger, more vibrant and true to type than tank-breds. However, they will also be more expensive and harder to keep as you will need to match your water parameters closely to those of their habitat. A better purchase for the beginner would be F1s – first generation tank-bred fish.

WHY should I learn the scientific name of a fish?

If your dealer does not have the fish you want he can usually order it for you. To be certain of getting the right fish you must quote the scientific name, not the common name. A term such as 'zebra fish' can apply to anything from cichlids to danios or catfish.

▼ *Harlequin rasboras (Trigonostigma heteromorpha). By acquiring immature shoaling fish in a small group, you can be sure of obtaining both sexes.*

Buying and introducing fish

CAN I change my mind about buying a fish?

Yes. Once your fish is netted, but before the bag is inflated with air/oxygen and knotted or secured with a rubber band, hold it up and examine the underside of the fish for signs of damage or infection. You may spot a problem that wasn't apparent when the fish was swimming in the sales tank. Hidden faults are especially likely with bottom-dwelling species.

WHY does the dealer inflate the bag?

Once your chosen fish is netted into the plastic bag, the dealer adds enough water to cover it. If your journey home is less than an hour, the fish will be fine with just air in the bag. If it is any longer, the bag should be filled with oxygen.

WHY does the dealer tape the corners of the bag?

Very small fish are at risk of becoming trapped and possibly crushed in the corners of the transit bag. Some dealers tape the corners to prevent this or wrap the fish in two bags.

CAN I transport a spiny fish in a plastic bag?

If you are buying fish with sharp fin spines, such as armoured catfishes, or teeth (piranha), bring along a white plastic bucket with a securely fitting lid to take them home in. Plastic bags are certain to be punctured in transit, even if the fish are double-bagged. Failing a bucket, a polystyrene fish box will do, although when partially filled with water it will be heavy to carry. You may need help with transportation.

DO I need a polystyrene box to transport my fish?

A lidded polystyrene box is useful if you are transporting several bags of fish, providing insulation and protection from light. Packing crumpled newspaper or empty inflated plastic bags between the fish bags prevents them rolling around. Put the box in your car boot or a rear footwell and drive home slowly, with no unnecessary stops along the way.

BAGGING UP A FISH

1 Take the opportunity to view fish from below to check that they are healthy and undamaged.

2 When you are satisfied, the dealer will tie a tight knot in the top of the bag, trapping air and water for the fishes' journey home.

3 To prevent fish being trapped in the corners, this dealer slides the upturned bag into a second bag, tucking in the corners.

4 Once inside the green bag, the fish travel in the dark to reduce stress. This dealer adds a care leaflet.

HOW many fish should I buy for my aquarium?

It depends on the size of your aquarium. Tank volume determines how many fish you can keep. An initial stocking guide is 2.5cm per 4.5 litres of fish length, excluding the tail. But this applies only to 'average-sized' fish (up to 4cm) in normally proportioned tanks. Weight-to-length ratio rises significantly after that, and larger fish produce more waste – so a 30cm Oscar needs more room that 12 neon tetras, each measuring 2.5cm. Remember that the fish in shops will probably be juveniles. Make due allowance for growth.

WHAT is the best way to transfer fish into a tank?

After a long journey home, open the bag, roll it down to form a collar and float it in the tank (with the lights off). Leave it just long enough for the temperature inside and outside the bag to equalise, then tilt it so that the occupants can swim out. Do not drop them into the tank from a great height! Make sure you have released all the fish.

CAN I pour the water from the transit bag into the tank?

Some fishkeepers will not tip transit water into their aquarium because it is ammonia-laden. However, unless you are unloading several large bags into a small tank, dilution and filtration will take care of any pollutants. The main concern is not to stress the fish, which you will do if you lift them out of their bags.

HOW will my existing fish react to newcomers?

It helps to rearrange the decor in your tank before introducing new fish. That way, any territorial occupants, such as the red-tailed black shark, will be preoccupied with the changes and less likely to bully the newcomers before they have a chance to settle in.

RELEASING THE FISH

1 Following a short journey home, float the unopened bags in the aquarium for about 20 minutes to allow the water temperatures to equalise before releasing the fish.

WHAT should I do if my new fish won't feed?

Don't worry if new introductions take a while to feed; they will be stressed by the move. The best thing is to leave them in peace for a day or so, with the lights out. If they are healthy specimens, missing a meal or two will do them no harm. Similarly, new fish may not show their best colours until they feel more confident in their new surroundings.

2 If the journey home was long, first roll down the sides of the bag to allow stale air to escape.

3 Holding the bag just below the water surface, tip it gently to encourage the fish to swim out.

Quarantining fish

▼ Temporarily house newly acquired fish in a quarantine tank.

▼ After quarantine is complete, introduce new fish into the existing community.

▼ Remove sick fish to a separate hospital tank for treatment.

▲ Each tank should have its own net and other equipment to prevent cross-contamination.

▲ The main display tank.

▲ A treatment tank is designed for easy treatment and cleaning.

DO I need to quarantine my new fish?

It is not necessary to quarantine the first fish you buy, since even if are carrying any disease organisms, there are no existing fish to pass them on to. However, second and subsequent fish additions could bring diseases into the display tank and not only succumb themselves, but also pass on the problem to existing healthy fish. These fish should be quarantined.

HOW do I set up a quarantine tank?

The tank need only be basic, with a heaterstat, simple internal filter and a refuge for the fish. A spell 'in solitary' is good insurance against introducing stress-related diseases such as whitespot to your main aquarium. And if a new fish does fall sick, it can be medicated in situ, avoiding possible side-effects to your existing stock.

HOW long should I leave my fish in quarantine?

Strictly speaking, you should keep a fish in isolation for longer than the longest incubation period of any disease organism that could affect it. In real terms, this could amount to a considerable period, as some viral diseases can lie dormant for a long time. For practical purposes, therefore, quarantine is dictated by the development period of the common pathogens most likely to affect aquarium fish. Generally speaking, 20 days is an ideal length of time to isolate new fish.

WHAT size should the quarantine tank be?

Depending on the size of the fish you intend to buy, a quarantine tank should measure at least 45x25x25cm. This will accommodate six 5cm-fish at any one time. If any individual fish is longer than 10cm, you will need a larger tank.

HOW do I look after the fish while they are in quarantine?

Once the fish are in the quarantine tank, care for them exactly as if they were in the main aquarium, with daily feeding, weekly water changes and other regular maintenance so that they remain in the best possible conditions.

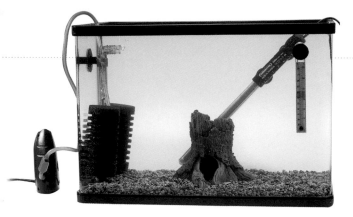

▲ *This typical quarantine tank contains a simple internal filter powered by an airpump, a heater-thermostat, a shallow bed of clean gravel, plus some artificial decor to provide a refuge for the fish.*

WHAT special equipment do I need?

Keep a separate supply of equipment for the quarantine tank and never transfer any items used in the quarantine tank to the main display aquarium. You can quite easily pass a pathogen from sick fish to your main display aquarium on a wet net. If you do need to use any equipment in both aquariums, be sure to disinfect it between each use.

WILL a dealer replace any fish that die?

When you buy your fish, ask the dealer whether the fish are guaranteed. A few shops operate an unconditional replacement policy on livestock that dies within a specified period (a few days at most), but the majority either do not guarantee their fish or insist that any casualties are brought back with a sample of your aquarium water for analysis to establish that it was not your poor husbandry that killed them.

WHAT sort of fish should I add to a newly set up tank?

There is always a chance that the first fish you introduce will be exposed to less-than-perfect water conditions as the tank matures, so it is important to select species that are known to be hardy. This means that they are able to tolerate changes in water quality – not that they should be expected to cope with poor water conditions.

HOW do I calculate the capacity of my aquarium?

You need to know the capacity of your aquarium when using medications. The length x the width x the depth in cm, divided by 1000, will give you the volume in litres. Allow approximately 10% for the space taken up by any simple decor and equipment.

CAN I use the quarantine tank for anything else?

A quarantine tank has many other uses. It is somewhere to house odd sick fish, bullied or harassed fish, baby fish or any tank inhabitants that cannot tolerate treatments being used in the main aquarium. Store the tank dry when not in use.

HOW do I tell if there is a problem in my tank?

It is normal to lose the occasional fish. This can be due to individual health problems or old age, and there is nothing to worry about. However, if you lose many fish suddenly (particularly of different species), this usually indicates an environmental problem. If you lose many fish gradually, this usually indicates a disease.

▼ *Cherry barbs are ideal 'starter' fish. Introduce them as a group.*

Compatibility

WHAT is a community aquarium?

In a community aquarium the fish are chosen because they behave peacefully towards one another and will happily share the same food, temperature and water conditions. In addition, they make full use of all the swimming space and water levels in the tank. Viewed together, their colours, body shapes and swimming habitats create a varied and dynamic aquarium display.

WHICH are the most peaceful community fish?

True community fishes remain compatible with others at all stages of their lives, but it is not always easy to assess this when you are buying them. Most farm-bed species are imported as youngsters, which have yet to develop possible aggressive or territorial traits associated with sexual maturity. As a rough guide, fishes that exercise no brood care (egg-scatterers) are likely to be the most peaceful – this includes barbs, danios and tetras.

HOW do I make a good choice of fish for my aquarium?

Firstly, find out all you can about a fish from magazines and books and by asking other fishkeepers or your dealer. Establish whether it is best kept in shoals, pairs or singly. Does it have any special requirements in terms of food or water quality? Always ask if the fish you want to buy is suitable for a community aquarium.

▲ If chosen with care, a selection of community fish will have similar requirements and co-exist peacefully.

▼ Bottom-feeding corydoras catfish, such as C. sterba, add movement to the lower area of the display.

WHAT is a species aquarium?

Fishes kept in a species aquarium may adapt to community life, but their individual requirements or anti-social behaviour are better catered for (or guarded against) in a separate aquarium. Some may need special care or have nocturnal habits.

WHAT if one of my fish starts to annoy the others?

Compatibility is not an exact science and some fish may display 'rogue' behaviour not typical of their species. For example, sucking loaches that develop a taste for the mucus of their tankmates. The only remedy is to move the offender to another tank or take it back to the shop.

HOW far ahead do I need to plan my fish selection?

When setting up a tank, it is worth thinking about any fish you may wish to add in future, as well as which ones to add first. Looking at the 'second' and 'third' options and deciding which ones you like, may help you decide on the first introductions, as they will all need to fit in together in the final display.

The first occupants to buy for a planted community tank are small and inexpensive algae-eaters, such as *Otocinclus affinis*. It is best to leave the largest fish till last, when the system is fully mature, otherwise they can place a strain on the filter. The list on the right reflects a selection of fish that could be added at different stages as the system matures. Always check on the water requirements and compatibility of fish added to a community aquarium.

ADDING FISH

First fish

Zebra, Leopard, Pearl danios

Black Widow, Lemon, Silver-tipped tetras

White Cloud Mountain minnow

Cherry, Golden barbs

Second fish

Arulius, Black Ruby, Black-spot, Blue-barred, Checker, Clown, Cuming's, Odessa, Pentazona, Rosy, Tiger barbs

Clown, Red-striped, Scissortail rasboras

Black Neon, Bleeding Heart, Buenos Aires, Cardinal, Congo, Emperor, Flame, Glowlight, Head-and-tail light, Neon, Serpae tetras

Croaking, Dwarf, Honey, Moonlight, Pearl, Snakeskin, Thick-lipped, Three-spot gouramis

Corydoras catfish as available, such as Bronze, Dwarf, Harald Schultz's, Panda, Peppered and Sterba's

Clown, Dwarf loaches

Guppy, Platy, Sailfin Molly, Swordtail

Third fish

Black Phantom, Red Phantom, Rummy Nose tetras

Laetacara dorsigera, Nanochromis parilus

Agassiz's Dwarf, Borelli's Dwarf, Checkerboard, Cockatoo Dwarf, Keyhole, Nijsseni's Dwarf, Striped Dwarf, Viejita Dwarf cichlids, Kribensis, Ram

Bristlenose ancistrus, Clown or Zebra plec

Glass, Twig, Whiptail catfishes

Hong Kong and Kuhli loaches

Banded, Boesman's, Red, Threadfin, Western and Neon Rainbowfishes

One-lined, Three-lined pencilfishes, Headstander, Marbled hatchetfish

Lyretail killifish

Siamese fighting fish (only one male to a tank)

Remember to check compatibility and water requirements of the fish.

◀ *Pentazona barbs (Barbus pentazona pentazona) do best in a group of five or six and are an excellent choice for all but the smallest community aquariums.*

Credits

Unless otherwise stated, photographs have been taken by Geoff Rogers © Interpet Publishing.

The publishers would like to thank the following photographers for providing images, credited here by page number and position: (B) Bottom, (T) Top, (C) Centre, (BL) Bottom left, etc.

Aqua Press (M-P & C Piednoir): 123(L), 123(R), 126, 129, 153, 156-157(B), 157(TR), 158, 159, 161, 189

Dave Bevan: 80

Ian Fuller: 78

Neil Hepworth: 44-45(B), 128

Ad Konings: 40-41(B), 41(TR), 41(CR), 47, 50

Photomax (Max Gibbs): 88, 90, 120, 122, 151, 182, 195

Iggy Tavares: 27

Publisher's acknowledgements

The publishers would like to thank the following for their help in providing facilities for photography:

Amwell Aquatics, Soham, Cambridgeshire.
Aquatic Warehouse, Enfield, Middlesex.
BAS, Bolton, Lancashire.
Betta Aquatics, Elmstead Market, Essex.
Adrian Burge, British Killifish Association.
Catfish Study Group (UK).
Keith Cocker, Norwich and District Aquarist Society.
Ely Aquatic Centre, Ely, Cambridgeshire.
Hertfordshire Fisheries, St. Albans, Hertfordshire.
Kesgrave Tropicals, Ipswich, Suffolk.
Maidenhead Aquatics, Crowland, Lincolnshire.
Maidenhead Aquatics, St. Albans, Hertfordshire.
Pier Aquatics, Wigan, Lancashire.
Colin and Kay Sargeant, Stowmarket, Suffolk.
Shirley Aquatics, Solihull, Warwickshire.
Shotgate Aquatics, Billericay, Essex.
Swallow Aquatics, Aldham, Colchester, Essex.
Swallow Aquatics, East Harling, Norfolk.
Swallow Aquatics, Rayleigh, Essex.
Swallow Aquatics, Southfleet, Kent.
Wharf Aquatics, Pinxton, Nottinghamshire.
Wholesale Tropicals, Bethnal Green, London.
Wildwoods Water Gardens, Enfield, Middlesex.

Publisher's note